CHILE

BY DAVID SCHAFFER

LUCENT BOOKS

An imprint of Thomson Gale, a part of The Thomson Corporation

Detroit • New York • San Francisco • San Diego • New Haven, Conn. • Waterville, Maine • London • Munich

To Nancy, with deep appreciation

On cover: The Andes Mountains in the distance form a backdrop to downtown Santiago.

© 2005 Thomson Gale, a part of The Thomson Corporation.

Thomson and Star Logo are trademarks and Gale and Lucent Books are registered trademarks used herein under license.

For more information, contact
Lucent Books
27500 Drake Rd.
Farmington Hills, MI 48331-3535
Or you can visit our Internet site at http://www.gale.com

LIBRARY OF CONGRESS CATALOGING-IN-PUBLICATION DATA

Schaffer, David.
  Chile / by David Schaffer.
    p. cm. — (Modern nations of the world)
  Includes bibliographical references and index.
  ISBN 1-59018-322-3 (hardcover : alk. paper)
  1. Chile—Juvenile literature. I. Title. II. Series.
  F3058.5.S44 2004
  983—dc22

                                                    2004008905

Printed in the United States of America

CONTENTS

Introduction

Chile: A Tale of People and Power

Located in southwestern South America, Chile has established itself as an economic and political leader among the nations of that continent. It ranks among the world's largest exporters of crops and minerals, and is also recognized as a center of artistic, literary, and musical culture and creativity. Up until the 1970s Chile had a record of successful democratic elections that had lasted 140 years. A history of commitment to social and economic progress among its people and, at times, among national government leaders has contributed largely to these Chilean successes. So too has an ethnic and cultural unity among Chileans, who are overwhelmingly—about 90 percent—of mixed European and Indian heritage. People with this combination of ancestry are known in South America as mestizos. They have always been the dominant group among the Chilean population, and Chile, unlike many other South American nations, has not been beset by racial and ethnic tensions.

That is not to say that Chile has always been peaceful and prosperous. In fact, Chile's history reflects periods of both turmoil and severe government repression. The worst of these periods occurred during the 1970s and 1980s, when a military coup deposed a democratically elected president in what proved to be the most deadly revolution ever staged in South America. An army general, Augusto Pinochet, seized power and ruled over one of the most brutal and repressive governments in the world at the time. Although democracy and political freedoms have been restored and Chile has become economically stronger since the time of the coup, the pain from that period continues to linger for many Chileans, especially those who were persecuted by the government.

A Progressive Tradition

The violent overthrow of Chile's government marked an extreme departure from a national trend toward increasing social activism and liberal economic reform. Like almost all nations in Latin America (consisting of South America, Central America, the Caribbean, and Mexico), Chile has historically been sharply unbalanced economically between the rich and the poor. In its early days wealthy landowners and industrialists held exclusive power, and the large majority of the population lived in poverty and without a voice in government. However, as Chile grew, large mineral deposits and strong trade relations with powerful European nations helped it gain economic prosperity, and the number of people who gained middle-class status economically slowly but steadily grew.

Along with their greater economic status, these people became better educated and more involved in Chile's political process, and they came to present a growing challenge to the ruling elites. A revolution in 1891 deposed the government that had been in control of Chile for most of the nineteenth century. The most important result of this revolution was that government power became concentrated in the congress, or

A vendor offering musical instruments and crafts for sale plays guitar inside his shop in Santiago, Chile's capital city.

Armed soldiers in General Augusto Pinochet's army ride atop tanks during the 1973 coup when Pinochet overthrew Chile's democratic government.

national legislature, instead of the office of the president, where it had been concentrated before.

Many Chileans hoped for improved living conditions and more representative government, but it turned out that the new government catered to its own narrow interest groups once it took power. Generally these groups consisted of the wealthy and powerful rivals of the landholders and industry owners who had been in control in the previous government. But the lower economic classes remained socially and politically active. The progressive social reform movements that were becoming influential in much of the world in the early twentieth century strongly impacted Chile, and many new political parties and workers' unions formed. These new groups were able to elect a progressive candidate, Arturo Alessandri, as president in the 1920s. Over the next several years Chile implemented far-reaching government measures to improve living conditions and expand power and participation in government among the people.

This progressivism yielded some decidedly positive results. Literacy and education rates increased, and participation in democratic elections, which occurred regularly and frequently, rose dramatically during the twentieth century. Yet the older and more conservative political parties also maintained significant power, as Chile remained a country with a distinctly superior economic class that continued to hold considerable sway in government and society. Although there were some periods of bitter political conflict, overall the rival factions followed and abided by free democratic processes. Chileans may have disagreed among themselves, even sharply at times, but they were able to live together peacefully and in stability. They enjoyed the image of their nation as a model of democracy and strength in Latin America.

A HISTORICAL ABERRATION

In other Latin American countries, revolutions and military dictatorships were common, and the violent military coup of 1973 that deposed Chile's democratic government was typical of the political instability that characterized much of that region. Yet the political unrest was shocking and traumatic for both Chileans and international observers. As history professor John Charles Chasteen said in his book *Born in Blood and Fire: A Concise History of Latin America*, "No other Latin American country could equal Chile's record of constitutional government. For years, Chilean democracy had negotiated major ideological differences."[1] The trauma grew as the Pinochet regime, after taking power, showed itself to be tyrannical. The number of Chileans who either vanished or were rounded up and tortured or killed reached the tens of thousands in the 1970s. Rights were suspended, political opposition was outlawed, and military rule was harshly imposed. After being spared from turbulent uprisings and civil conflicts for almost its entire history, Chile experienced South America's most violent government overthrow.

Eventually, both internal dissent and international pressure led Pinochet to ease authoritarian restrictions and, ultimately, to restore civil rule. Democratic governments have once again ruled Chile since 1989, and press and political freedoms have also been restored. Economically Chile had become impressively strong by the end of the twentieth century. But the suffering and personal loss that many Chileans experienced during Pinochet's rule continue to be painful. Other serious concerns face Chile as well. Some observers have noted that interest and involvement with the political process among Chileans, which had grown so dramatically and attained such high levels before the 1973 coup, declined following the restoration of democracy. Others point to a decline in Chilean culture, which has been increasingly

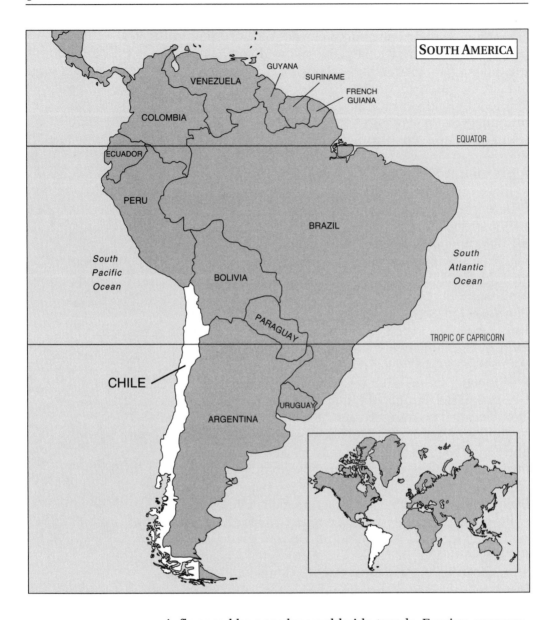

influenced by popular worldwide trends. Foreign commercial and business interests, especially from the United States, have also had an increasing presence in Chile both during and following Pinochet's reign. These developments have led to concern about the future of Chile's cultural identity. Although Chile has much working in its favor, it nevertheless faces challenges as a growing and emerging nation in the twenty-first century.

THE CONTINENT'S EDGE

Chile is a large country; it covers an area of 292,260 square miles. That area is distributed in a most unusual way. From north to south, Chile measures 2,650 miles, extending from about 390 miles north of the Tropic of Capricorn (close to the equator) to less than 900 miles north of the Antarctic Circle. Yet from east to west, Chile is only 265 miles at its widest point and averages only 110 miles wide throughout its territory. This makes Chile one of the longest and narrowest nations in the world. The authors of *Chile: A Country Study* detail further how Chile's geography makes it an unusual place: "Within its territory can be found a broad selection of the Earth's climates. For this reason, geographically it is possible to speak of several Chiles."[2]

The nation is generally divided into five north-to-south regions: the Far North, the Near or Small North, Central Chile, South Central Chile, and the Far South or Archipelago. Areas of the north are near tropical or subtropical, while mountain peaks in the south remain snow covered nearly year-round and glaciers flow through Chile into the Pacific Ocean.

Another factor greatly affecting Chile's geography is dramatic differences of elevation within its narrow confines. The four distinct areas of elevation within Chile between the west coast and the eastern border are the coastal lowland, the coastal cordillera or mountain range, the altiplano or high plain, and the Andes. Elevations climb from sea level to peaks of over twenty thousand feet. *The Cambridge Encyclopedia of Latin America and the Caribbean* states, "There may be three or four types of climate within a horizontal distance of only 40 km [25 miles]."[3] Indeed, extreme differences in latitude and elevation create huge variations of climate and topography within short distances inside Chile.

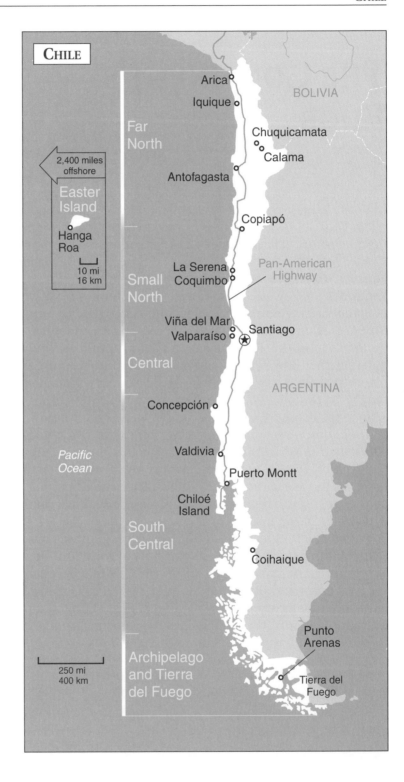

CHILE

Arica
Iquique
BOLIVIA

Far
North

Chuquicamata
Calama

2,400 miles
offshore

Antofagasta

Easter
Island

Copiapó

Hanga
Roa

10 mi
16 km

Small
North

La Serena
Coquimbo

Pan-American
Highway

Viña del Mar
Valparaíso

Santiago

Central

ARGENTINA

Concepción

Pacific
Ocean

Valdivia

Puerto Montt

Chiloé
Island

South
Central

Coihaique

Punto
Arenas

250 mi
400 km

Archipelago
and Tierra
del Fuego

Tierra del
Fuego

THE FAR NORTH (NORTE GRANDE)

The most prominent feature of Chile's Far North is the Atacama Desert. This desert has the distinction of being the driest in the world. Some parts of it never receive rainfall, and even the moistest areas generally get no more than about an inch per year. Some places in the Atacama receive moisture from fog off the ocean. Oases called *lomas* form at these spots, attracting creatures such as hummingbirds that are usually only found in moister tropical climates. A few people have even taken up crop growing and herding in these areas. Temperatures in this region average around 70°F during the summer (January–February) and between 55°F and 60°F in the winter (July–August).

With much of the land in the Far North so barren, the largest population concentrations are along the coast. Arica and Antofagasta are two large port cities on the Pacific in this region. They served the mining industry that developed in the Andes Mountains in northern Peru following the conquest of the area by the Spanish. Silver and tin have both been major products of this area. The world's largest opencast copper mine is located in this area at Chuquicamata. Over three hundred tons of copper ore are shipped out of the mine daily. The village of Humberstone, which was once a bustling mining center, is now a ghost town, although the buildings that remain standing attract curious visitors.

With Mount Sajama in the background, a herd of vicuña makes its way across the rocky terrain of Parque Nacional Lauca in the Far North.

Remains from even earlier times can be found in the Atacama. The indigenous civilizations that thrived in the northern Andes in precolonial times did not reach very far into Chile, but remnants of these civilizations can be found in the Norte Grande. Geoglyphs, giant figures carved into the landscape, are found near the towns of Calama and Iquique. An Inca fortress and other ruins are also found near the eastern town of San Pedro de Atacama.

The Far North also features many natural wonders, highlighted by two major nature preserves. One is the large Parque Nacional Lauca, which contains a typical high Andean plain environment featuring lush lakes and giant peaks, including some volcanic ones. Animal life in the park is bountiful: More than a hundred species of birds live there, including the Andean condor, the world's largest vulture. The South American cousins of camels, which include llamas, alpacas, guanacos, and vicuñas, are also present in the park. These animals originated in the Andes area and have been exported worldwide. Jaguars, the one South American variety of big cat, are also found in the park. Much more desolate is the Valle de la Luna, or Valley of the Moon, so named because its topography is stunningly similar to the landscape of the moon. Deposits of salt and clay spread over the land create this effect. The Valley of the Moon is flat and fully devoid of any plant and animal life.

Another geological wonder in the Norte Grande is El Tatio, which features over one hundred hot water geysers that erupt daily, usually around sunrise. El Tatio is located on a high mountain plain, northeast of the Atacama Desert.

THE SMALL NORTH (NORTE CHICO)

South of the desert, the climate gets less arid. Rainfall comes almost exclusively in winter, but it does total as much as five inches per year near the coast. Temperatures average about 65°F in summer and 55°F in winter. As in the Far North, most of the population is concentrated along the coast. However, settlement and modern development can be found in the inland areas as well.

With a somewhat moister and more temperate climate than the Far North, the Small North has more fertile land. The major river valleys in this region are increasingly used for agriculture rather than mining, which was the basis of the

region's early economies. The rapid growth of Chile's agriculture export business during the twentieth century has led to the increase in agricultural production in this area. Because rainfall is limited, irrigation is a big part of crop growing in many places in the Norte Chico. However, high elevation areas near the coast are moist enough to support dense growth forests. Hardwood trees called espinos and algarobbos are common in these forests, which are among the few original growth forests in South America. Most others were cut down during the early colonial period.

The environment in the Norte Chico is conducive to other activities besides growing crops and trees. The high Andes area of this region is a major center for astronomical observatories. Three large and renowned observatories, and a few smaller ones, can be found in this area. The high elevations, usually clear skies, and rural setting with very low light pollution (levels of artificial lighting) make this a prime viewing area for astronomers. Many different nations and international organizations support and maintain the observatories.

La Serena, the principal city in the area, was founded during the earliest days of Spanish settlement in Chile in the sixteenth century. Today it is a regional capital and a popular resort destination for people living in the large metropolitan

On a mountaintop in the Andes a hundred miles north of La Serena, La Silla Observatory is far from any artificial light and dust sources, astronomy's worst enemies.

areas in Central Chile. Like Coquimbo, another seaside city just to the south, La Serena was an important port for Chile's mining industry and is now also a major transit point for agricultural products grown in the area. Many of northern Chile's best beaches are located near Coquimbo and La Serena. These cities also have major fishing industries, as do most Chilean cities along the Pacific coast.

Remains of ancient Indian cultures are contained at national monuments in this region. These remains date back as far as two thousand years. They include petroglyphs—carvings and drawings made on rocks—and giant boulders ceremoniously placed by indigenous peoples.

CENTRAL CHILE

Chile's Central Valley and coast are the most populated, developed, and industrialized areas in the country. Although it takes up only about a fifth of Chile's land, the central region contains about 70 percent of its population. Early European settlers were attracted to the Central Valley in particular because of the temperate climates year-round. Temperatures in this area closely resembled the Mediterranean climates the settlers were used to in Spain. Temperatures average about 65°F to 70°F during the summer and about 45°F to 50°F in the winter. Annual rainfall ranges from about twelve inches in the valley to about twenty inches on the coast. With high Andes peaks to the east and the warm ocean waters to the west, Central Chile is one of the few places in the world where both beach-going and downhill skiing are popular activities during much of the year.

The main road through Chile, the Pan-American Highway, passes through the Central Valley, as do the main rail lines that connect Chile internally and with other South American nations. The nation's major international airport is also located in the Central Valley, along with the capital and largest city, Santiago. The next three largest cities in Chile are located close by, on the central Pacific coast. Agriculture, industry, business, and government are all concentrated in this area. Both geographically and figuratively, Central Chile is the heart of the nation.

SANTIAGO

Santiago, with a population of about 6 million, is a world-class city in every respect. It is the nation's business, cultural, educational, and entertainment center, as well as its seat of government.

Santiago is among South America's most sophisticated and lively cities. The city's cultural highlights include the Museum of Pre-Columbian Chilean Art, the Museum of Colonial Art, and the Ralli Museum, which features contemporary art from around the world. The Chilean Academy of Painting in Santiago has schooled many native painters and given rise to a rich tradition of Chilean fine art. Both the city of Santiago and the nation of Chile sponsor orchestras and ballet troupes that are based in Santiago. Chile's national university is also within the city. The main thoroughfares of the city are lined with upscale shops, restaurants, and nightclubs, and the plazas and squares have been designed and built in elegant Spanish colonial style.

Santiago's city center is a testament to the spirit and affluence of Chile, but increasingly another aspect of Chilean society has become more apparent in Santiago. Large numbers of poor rural people, unable to find work to provide a living in the country, have been flocking to the cities and settling in shantytowns around the outskirts. These makeshift settlements

The Plaza de la Constitución lies at the heart of the capital city of Santiago, Chile's business, cultural, and educational center.

are referred to as *poblaciones callampas*. This is Spanish for "mushroom villages," the name deriving from the manner in which the settlements spring up suddenly and unexpectedly like mushrooms. These shantytowns serve as a visible reminder that severe differences in the living standards of the rich and poor have historically been a problem in Chile and continue to be so.

CENTRAL COASTAL CITIES

Chile's next three biggest cities are also all located in the central region, but along the Pacific coast instead of the valley. All are much smaller than Santiago, with populations ranging from three hundred thousand to four hundred thousand.

Viña del Mar and Valparaíso are adjacent to each other, lying about seventy miles west of Santiago. Valparaíso was founded in 1541 and was a major port throughout the colonial period and into the twentieth century, when ships from the United States had to travel around the southern tip of South America to get from the east coast of North America to the west coast. When the Panama Canal opened in 1914, creating a route through Central America, ships no longer

Until the completion of the Panama Canal in 1914, Valparaíso was one of South America's principal commercial ports.

needed to travel all the way around South America. Valparaíso then declined in importance, and the great wealth the city once experienced waned. Some beautiful mansions and ornate public buildings still remain, but unlike in Santiago, where the rich and poor are sharply segregated, poor housing and decaying buildings lie adjacent to the gleaming, well-constructed structures within the city center. The *Footprint South American Guide* describes the hillsides of the city as being covered with "fine mansions, tattered houses and shacks, scrambled in . . . confusion along the narrow back streets."[4] Recent efforts have attempted to restore Valparaíso to the splendor it enjoyed earlier in its history. For example, in the early 1990s Chile's congressional building was moved from Santiago to Valparaíso in an attempt to improve the city's image.

Just to the north of Valparaíso is Viña del Mar. As Valparaíso has lost wealth and importance, many middle-class Chileans have relocated from there to Viña del Mar. Golf courses, exclusive dining clubs, and sporting clubs are all prominent in this city. Some of Chile's largest and most popular beaches are located here as well.

About three hundred miles to the south lies the city of Concepción, a major shipping port for Chile's vast array of agricultural products. It was originally founded in 1550 and was the site of a major battle between early Spanish settlers and southern Indians shortly thereafter. Concepción is located at the mouth of the Bio-Bio River, which is generally considered the southern end of Central Chile. It receives considerably more rain than the large cities to the north, averaging over fifty inches per year, almost all of which falls during the cool months of April through September.

THE SOUTH CENTRAL REGION
Farther south is the South Central region, also known as the Lake Region. The natural scenery in this area is renowned for its spectacular beauty. South Central Chile has ten national parks, making it among the most preserved areas in South America. Most of Chile's largest lakes lie in this region. They are fed by rivers that flow from glaciers high up in the Andes. The region has waterfalls and snowcapped mountains, including the largest number of active volcanoes in any Chilean region. The perfectly coned-shaped Osorno peak

Villarica Volcano in Chile's southcentral region known as the Lake Region towers more than nine thousand feet above Villarica Lake.

towers over Chile's largest lake, Llanquihue, creating a wondrous visual effect. Besides the lush rivers and lakes and spiraling mountains, large tracts of old growth forests can be found along the coastal mountains. These include a significant number of trees unique to southern South America. Among these are the araucaria, also called the monkey puzzle tree. Its branches grow in overlapping and contorted patterns, and it got its name because an early English explorer in Chile thought such a tree would present difficulties for any monkey trying to climb it, although there are no monkeys in the areas where the trees grow naturally. Another notable tree that grows exclusively in this area is the alerce, a relative of the giant redwood tree. Alerces grow hundreds of feet tall, and some live for thousands of years.

Temperatures in the South Central region average around 60°F in summer and 45°F in winter. Rainfall along the coast here usually exceeds one hundred inches per year. Crops are grown in some of the lower-lying areas of the South Central region that are very similar to those grown in the Central Valley to the north. Cattle herding and dairy farming are important to the northern part of the region, as is trout and salmon fish farming. Recreational freshwater fishing is also a popular attraction.

The tribe that originally dominated this region was the Mapuche. Although their culture and people have been largely eliminated from Chile, a strong Mapuche presence remains in the South Central city of Temuco, where traditional Mapuche crafts are sold in many of the shops and marketplaces. Traditional Chilean cowboys, called *huasos*, bring cattle into the center of town to auction them. Most Chilean *huasos* are of Mapuche origin.

An interesting demographic aspect of the South Central region is the presence of a significant number of people of German descent. Many Germans migrated to this area in the nineteenth century, and many towns and neighborhoods came to be characterized by distinctively German styles and characteristics. The town of Osorno is architecturally and culturally strongly influenced by the German population. A German newspaper is still published in the city of Valdivia. One particularly German town, Puerto Montt, became a major fishing center and a transport point for travel to Chile's southernmost section, the Archipelago, or Far South.

THE ARCHIPELAGO AND TIERRA DEL FUEGO

South of Puerto Montt, Chile's geography becomes stunningly dramatic. Jagged mountain peaks thousands of feet high rise up right alongside the ocean. This area receives over one hundred inches of rain per year. It is also quite cold in the Far South, as the closeness of this area to the South Pole, combined with harsh Pacific winds, makes for some extreme weather and climate conditions. Temperatures average only 53°F in summer and 39°F in winter. The high elevations often receive significant snowfall, but the most dramatic sign of the near-polar conditions in the Far South of Chile is the presence of large glaciers. One flows into Laguna San Rafael, the location of a national park. In the Torres del Paine National Park, glaciers connect with icebergs in the ocean.

An area called the Archipelago covers about one thousand miles between Puerto Montt and Cape Horn on the southern tip of South America. The western part of the Archipelago

THE PACIFIC RING OF FIRE

Chile lies along what is known as the Pacific Ring of Fire or Pacific Rim, an area surrounding the Pacific Ocean that runs from New Zealand and Asia across the Pacific and down the west coasts of North and South America. In total the ring extends about twenty-five thousand miles and is marked by a high frequency of volcanic eruptions and earthquakes. In fact, more than half of the world's active volcanoes lie along its course. The movement of tectonic plates, large pieces of the earth's outer crust upon which islands and continents rest, causes the turbulent activity along the Pacific Ring of Fire.

Chile has experienced serious natural disasters because of its location. The worst earthquake ever to occur along the rim hit Chile in 1960. Registering 8.75 on the Richter scale, the quake triggered a series of volcanic eruptions and a tidal wave, killing at least several hundred people and causing devastation along a long stretch of the country. The coastal cities of Concepción and Valdivia were severely hurt, and some smaller towns and villages were destroyed completely. Concepción had previously been totally destroyed in an earthquake in 1751, and Valparaíso was almost destroyed by a massive quake in 1906. Chile has about fifty active volcanoes. In 1963 the peak Villarica erupted, causing major mud slides that buried farms and settlements.

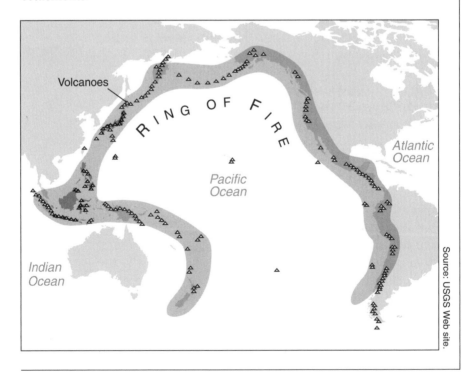

Source: USGS Web site.

consists mainly of a chain of islands that runs from Chiloé, at the northern end of the Archipelago, to Tierra del Fuego, an island at the end of the continent that Chile shares with neighboring Argentina. Both of these islands are connected to the mainland by roads. To the east lie peninsulas, narrow ocean inlets called fjords, treacherous mountain peaks, and densely wooded forests. A recently built road runs south of Puerto Montt along the mainland for about seven hundred miles to the regional capital of Coihaique. In much of the rest of the Archipelago, natural boundaries prevent any type of passage other than by boat or, in some places, airplane.

Jagged, barren peaks rise above the clouds in the Torres del Paine National Park in the Far South.

Although tourism is a major industry in parts of the Archipelago, many of the small isolated communities are mostly self-sustaining, relying on fishing and small-scale crop growing. Indian crafts on Chiloé, especially weavings and basketware, are widely noted for their high quality. On the island of Tierra del Fuego, sheep herding is a major source of income, and foreigners from a variety of countries, particularly Britain, have come there to pursue this trade.

Some animal species in the Far South are markedly distinctive from animal life in the regions to the north, and animals unique to this area share some similarities with the fauna found in the South Pacific islands, particularly Australia and New Zealand. A member of the ostrich family called a rhea, similar to land birds found in Australia, inhabits the interior plains of southern Chile and Argentina. Another inhabitant in these southern mountains that resembles an Australian animal is the marsupial monkey. This species carries its young in a pouch, as kangaroos do. The rocky shores of the islands and mainland close to Antarctic waters are home to animals typical of polar climates, such as seals and penguins.

CHILE'S PACIFIC ISLANDS

Two island territories in the Pacific Ocean are also part of Chile. Easter Island, about twenty-four hundred miles east of North Central Chile, has long been famous for its ancient and mysterious civilization. Most likely the Rapa Nui, the people who formed the Easter Island civilization, originated in the Polynesian islands of the South Pacific, but no one is certain exactly where they came from. They had the distinction of being the only known ancient people in the Americas or the South Pacific to possess a written language. They have been best known for the construction of massive stone structures called *moai*, giant carved faces weighing thousands of pounds that were perched upon stone platforms. No evidence has been found to indicate how the Rapa Nui managed to move the structures or hoist them onto their platforms, adding to the mystery surrounding the island and the Rapa Nui.

The Juan Fernández islands, much closer to the mainland at only four hundred miles west of Central Chile, are uninhabited outside of the village of San Juan Bautista. These islands are a Chilean national park as well as a United Nations

A gaucho on horseback herds his sheep, an important source of income on the island of Tierra del Fuego.

THE *MOAI* OF EASTER ISLAND

Located about twenty-two hundred miles west of the Chilean mainland, Easter Island is a place of natural beauty and mystery. It is uncertain how the inhabitants of the island, known as the Rapa Nui, came to be there, although the most widely accepted theory is that they migrated by small boats from South Pacific islands farther to the west.

The most well-known feature of Easter Island are the *moai*—giant sculptured heads made from volcanic rock that were discovered perched upon large stone platforms. With the *moai* reaching heights of seventy feet and some weighing over one hundred tons, how they were moved and elevated onto the platforms has remained a mystery. The original purpose of the *moai* has also never been discovered. The most accepted theory is that they are meant to depict religious idols. Many of the *moai* were found knocked off their platform and lying on the ground. A number of them have been re-

placed and restored, and Easter Island is now a Chilean national park that draws many visitors curious to witness its mysterious volcanic sculptures.

No one knows how or for what reason the stone moai *on Easter Island were erected.*

designated natural reserve. However, their greatest claim to fame is the fact that one of the islands served as the inspirational setting for the novel *Robinson Crusoe*, written by English author Daniel Defoe in the early eighteenth century. Defoe based his book on the actual experiences of a sailor named Alexander Selkirk, who was marooned on a Pacific island, just as the title character was in *Robinson Crusoe*. The largest of the three Juan Fernández islands is named Robinson Crusoe Island, in honor of the book that made the islands so famous.

In spite of the vastness and disparity of Chile's climates and environments, it has nevertheless forged a singular, unified identity as a country. Chile's history is a story of a nation forming, emerging, and growing strong in spite of significant regional geographic differences.

2

Ancient Empires, Spanish Colonialism, and Early Independence

Because of its rugged terrain and remote location, Chile largely avoided coming under the domination of the Inca Empire, which ruled much of South America in the fifteenth and sixteenth centuries. Spanish colonists, who conquered the Incas and ruled most of South America from the sixteenth to the nineteenth centuries, made greater inroads in Chile. But the Spanish did not succeed in fully conquering the territory either, and under both the Incas and the Spanish, Chile was largely just a frontier outpost. However, upon gaining independence, Chile asserted itself militarily and underwent strong, rapid economic growth, becoming one of South America's most powerful and prosperous nations. The progressive political tradition that would prove to be so important to Chile's history also took root in the early years of independence.

The Earliest Chileans

The earliest inhabitants of Chile, who were nomadic hunters and gatherers, have been traced back to about 14,000 B.C. An early civilization called the Chinchorro were prevalent in Chile from around 8000 to 1000 B.C. The Chinchorro were hunters and gatherers, but their diet also relied heavily on fish and shellfish. Another notable feature of the Chinchorro was their custom of mummifying their dead. Chinchorro mummies discovered in archaeological digs are considered the oldest mummies in the world. Another ancient civilization, the Atacameño lived in the northern desert sections of

Chile. They left their mark on the land in the form of geo-glyphs scattered over a wide area.

By the fifteenth century there were three principal Indian groups in Chile, all of whom spoke the same language and were part of a larger tribal group known as the Araucanians. These were the Picunches, or men of the north; Mapuches, or men of the land; and Huilliches, or men of the south. When the Inca Empire, based in the Andes of Peru, rose to power in the fifteenth century, Incas came to control much of northern and western South America. The Incas largely subdued the Picunches in the north but met with fierce resistance from the Mapuches. The Incas penetrated to the River Maule, about midway between Chile's northern and

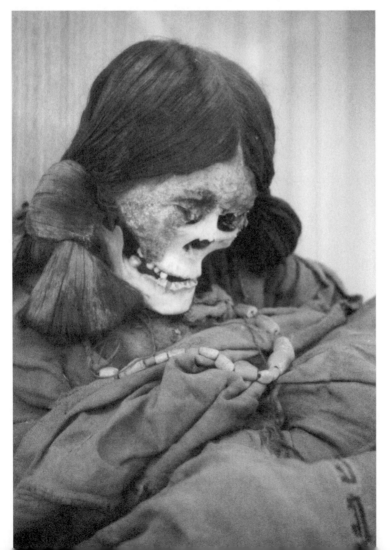

Pictured is the mummified body of a woman from the Atacameño civilization, an ancient Chilean people.

In 1520 Ferdinand Magellan leads his fleet through the treacherous strait that today bears his name.

southern borders, and although they built roads and established forts, they were unable to maintain control over much of Chile outside of the northernmost Andes.

SPANISH CONQUEST AND SETTLEMENT

The first European to sight Chile—although he never set foot on its shore—was Ferdinand Magellan, a Portuguese sailor who voyaged around the southern tip of South America from the Atlantic to the Pacific Ocean. The passage between the mainland and the island Tierra del Fuego, the Strait of Magellan, is named after him.

The Spanish became the first Europeans to explore and settle in Chile. After Spanish warriors, commonly called conquistadores, defeated the Incas in 1533, an expedition headed by Diego de Almagro went to Chile from Peru in 1535. The Spanish in the Americas were largely driven to conquest and colonization by a desire for gold, silver, and other precious minerals. Almagro found no such minerals in Chile, but he did meet with violence and resistance from the Indians he encountered there. By 1537 Almagro had returned to Peru without having established any Spanish presence or settlement in Chile.

Permanent Spanish settlement came in 1541, when Pedro de Valdivia established the city of Santiago in the Central Valley. Unlike Almagro, Valdivia did find gold and silver deposits in the south of Chile, which fueled Spanish interest and further settlement in the area. Valdivia soon realized that these resources were limited compared with those in other places in the Spanish American colonies. However, the fertile lands of the Central Valley provided an obvious site for raising crops, and Chile's southern and western coasts made it a good strategic location for defending against other European nations competing with Spain for territory in the Americas. Chile became a colonial region under the control of the viceroyalty of Peru, one of the major centers of Spanish government in the American colonies. Valdivia was appointed the governor of Chile.

This church in the coastal town of La Serena is one of many the Spanish built in Chile during the colonial period.

Although the Spanish were able to subdue the remaining Indian populations in North and Central Chile, the Mapuches, who had successfully resisted the Inca incursions, proved equally formidable against the Spanish. In a major uprising in 1553, the Mapuches overran a Spanish fort and captured and killed Valdivia. A Mapuche chief named Lautaro gained legendary status for his success in leading this attack against the Spanish. He continued to fiercely fight the Spanish until he was killed in 1558. After Lautaro's death the Spanish managed to mostly secure their territory, although occasional raids occurred throughout the colonial period. Spain never could wrest control of the area south of the Bio-Bio River from the Mapuches.

British, French, and Dutch explorers and colonialists also posed challenges to Spanish control of Chile. Yet in spite of threats and harassment from the native Indian population and other Europeans, the Spanish colony of Chile stabilized into a distinctive entity and became an important part of the Spanish Empire, supplying the Spanish colonies and homeland with important minerals and agricultural products. Although Chile was under the full authority of the colonial capital in Peru, the culture and social structure that would come to define it as a nation took form during the sixteenth century.

Agriculture dominated Chile's economy during colonial times. Large plantations known as haciendas became the principal producers of Chilean crops. These plantations were large, sometimes thousands of acres, and were worked by sharecroppers, indentured servants, or slaves. Initially Indians and slaves imported from Africa were used as laborers on the haciendas, but most of the work was done by mestizos, people of mixed European and American Indian descent. The owners of the land, who were almost entirely of sole European descent, became very powerful in Chilean society, joining mine owners and high-ranking government officials as members of Chile's elite. The great number of people who worked on the haciendas, on the other hand, lived mostly in poverty and struggled to survive, becoming the biggest segment of Chile's poor.

Among the ruling class were many native Spaniards, and Spain maintained its domination over Chile even as increasing numbers of native Chileans joined the controlling elites. Trade was strictly regulated, and Chileans were required to trade almost exclusively with their ruling viceroyalty in Peru. Spain also imposed taxes, controlled land distribution, and had authority to issue licenses and permits to merchants and business owners. Hence Spain remained largely in control of Chile's wealth and resources.

THE FIGHT FOR INDEPENDENCE

As was the case in many European colonies in the Americas, many people in Chile became increasingly dissatisfied with being under the rule of a faraway nation. Those who sought greater freedom for Chile won some favor from new rulers who took over Spain in the late eighteenth century. Greater independence for Chile was granted in a series of measures known as the Bourbon Reforms, which were named after the new ruling family that implemented them. Chile was able to trade freely with colonies other than Peru and even with other nations; the government at Santiago was given more administrative power over Chile's affairs; and Chile's military forces were strengthened. A major figure in the enactment of the Bourbon Reforms in Chile was Ambrosio O'Higgins, who was governor from 1788 to 1796. He promoted Chilean self-reliance and outlawed forced labor, which had been widespread on haciendas and in the mines.

Support for outright independence for Chile rose again in the early nineteenth century, when Spain was conquered by the French forces of Napoleón Bonaparte in Europe, and Spanish colonies everywhere had to decide whether to be loyal to the newly imposed foreign rulers, affirm loyalty to the deposed Spanish king, or declare their independence. Although there was some sentiment toward becoming fully independent, on September 18, 1810, the leaders of Chile declared loyalty to the deposed King Ferdinand but also decreed to govern Chile independently until the king could be restored to power. Although this was not a full declaration of independence, and actual independence for Chile would not come until several years later after a long, arduous process, Chileans nevertheless celebrate September 18 as their independence day.

Conflict among those who had decreed Chilean independence badly hindered their ability to manage the country. The first leader, José Miguel Carrera, had a military background and was a highly authoritarian ruler. He favored maintaining the existing political and social order and did not want or expect permanent independence from Spain. Another independence leader, Bernardo O'Higgins, son of the reformist governor Ambrosio O'Higgins, led another faction that favored full independence. The differences between these factions simmered even as they battled together against Spanish loyalists, but tensions eventually mounted to the point where forces loyal to O'Higgins and Carrera battled each other for control of the capital. All the while, forces

BERNARDO O'HIGGINS

Born in 1788 in Chillán, Chile, Bernardo O'Higgins was the son of former Chilean governor Ambrosio O'Higgins. He was schooled in Peru and England before returning to Chile in 1811. While in England O'Higgins was exposed to ideas concerning national independence and representative government that he found attractive. Upon his return to Chile, he became a leading proponent of independence for Chile.

While O'Higgins was committed to the idea of full independence for Chile, especially after the seizure of Spain by Napoleón, he faced opposition from other Chileans who saw self-rule for Chile as temporary until the legitimate Spanish king could be restored. One such person was José Miguel Carrera, a military officer who had fought for Spain against Napoleon before returning to Chile. Carrera and O'Higgins became rivals for control over Chile's provisional government during the war with Spain. This divisiveness among Chileans was a major contributing factor in Spain's Reconquest of Chile in 1814.

O'Higgins was able to get along much better with the Argentinean José de San Martín, who shared O'Higgins's vision for independence for South America from its European rulers. The partnership they formed after O'Higgins fled from Chile into Argentina following the Spanish Reconquest proved to be crucial to the emergence of South America's Spanish colonies as independent nations.

Bernardo O'Higgins played a pivotal role in helping Chile to achieve independence from Spain.

loyal to Spain were receiving reinforcements from Peru to put down the Chilean nationals. The divided independence forces tried to reunite to withstand the Spanish offensive but were unable to defeat the larger and superior forces amassed against them. Spain took back control of Chile in what has come to be known as the Reconquest. O'Higgins and Carrera both retreated into exile.

O'Higgins joined forces with another proponent of South American independence from Spain, Argentinean José de San Martín, and prepared to launch a counterattack against the Spanish and their loyalists to take back Chile. The independence forces were helped by brutal and repressive policies employed by the restored Spanish government against the Chilean population. A newly created Spanish police force arbitrarily arrested and beat anyone suspected of opposing Spanish rule or otherwise posing a problem for the government. Such callousness led to deeper and more widespread resentment of Spanish rule among Chileans, and helped the independence forces gain greater support and strength among the population.

After collaborating for two years at a remote base in Argentina, O'Higgins and Carrera led their combined forces in a stunning march across the massive peaks of the Andes. Pro-independence forces took the Spanish by surprise on February 12, 1817, and defeated them in the Battle of Chacabuco. The Spanish rulers quickly fled from Santiago, and O'Higgins took over the national government. Spanish forces continued to occupy large parts of Chile and fight ongoing battles against Chilean nationalists for another year before being decisively defeated in the battle of Maipo in April 1818. Spanish forces remained in parts of southern Chile and on the coastal islands in the Pacific for several more years. Yet O'Higgins signed another declaration of independence, this time proclaiming Chile's full and permanent independence from Spain, even while his armies were still driving the Spanish out of the main part of Chile.

CONTINUING CIVIL CONFLICT

O'Higgins faced trouble from his fellow Chileans almost immediately after vanquishing the Spanish threat. Like his father, O'Higgins was reform minded. He made several moves that distressed or angered Chile's elite, such as allowing the practice of religions other than Catholicism in the country, something vehemently opposed by the Catholic Church, to which the overwhelming majority of Chile's people belonged. The elimination of royal titles for Chileans was also opposed by many wealthy and powerful people, as was O'Higgins's plans to make it easier for rural peasants to obtain their own plots of land. O'Higgins even had problems with those who shared his reformist views, because he employed a governing style that was dictatorial even as he sought to expand rights and opportunities among all Chile's people.

An initial constitution implemented in 1818, and another more permanent one adopted in 1822, were both created solely by O'Higgins, and both documents bestowed upon him broad and overruling powers.

Following the introduction of the 1822 constitution, a revolt against O'Higgins developed, led by Ramón Friere, the mayor of the city of Concepción, and supported by many of Chile's ruling class within Santiago. Pressed by an advancing rebellious army led by Friere and urgent requests from other leaders that he step down, O'Higgins voluntarily relinquished power on January 28, 1823.

A period of chaos and instability followed O'Higgins's departure. A succession of presidents served, with Friere serving the longest, but no one managed to effectively control the country. Factional conflict arose between those favoring stronger central national government and those favoring a federal system that based greater power in local regions. A constitution adopted in 1828 that attempted to reconcile both sides instead caused them both discontent. Taxes imposed by the government to fund services and public works also caused widespread resentment among the population. The overall situation in Chile deteriorated severely during this time.

Just how bad things became is described by Spanish language professor and writer Guillermo I. Castillo-Feliú in his book *Culture and Customs of Chile:*

> Two political parties struggled for power and political direction. On one side were the conservatives . . . defenders of traditional principles, among them the privileges of the Church. The other faction, known as the *pipiolos* (upstarts or novices), supported liberal or federalist policies. Anarchy ruled, however, for factions developed within these two parties. Consequently, there followed a period marked by a quick succession of presidents and constitutions, accompanied by opposing armies supporting one faction or another. At the same time, bandits roamed the countryside almost unchecked.[5]

Responding to this chaotic state of affairs, conservatives, who favored maintaining the power structure established during colonial times, moved to impose their own rule upon Chile.

DIEGO PORTALES

Born in Santiago in 1793, Diego Portales, who would have great influence upon the state of Chile for most of the nineteenth century, was the son of a royal officer. Although his family had been deeply involved in Chilean politics since the seventeenth century, Portales originally went into business, operating a trading company in Valparaíso. In *A History of Chile, 1808–1994*, Simon Collier and William F. Slater describe Portales' personality and character in conflicted terms:

> Away from his business, he was a devotee of lighthearted sociability, fond of guitar playing and female company. The public face was very different: the sarcastic hedonist became the austere servant of the state. His political ideas were simple. "A strong, centralizing government whose members are genuine examples of virtue and patriotism."

Collier and Slater go on to say that once the conservatives took over the government following the civil war and Portales assumed important ministry positions, "nobody was allowed to stand in his way." He forged his ideas and will upon the people and government of Chile, and his legacy was enduring. Portales himself, however, was assassinated by a political opponent in 1837.

THE RISE OF DIEGO PORTALES

In 1830 hard-line conservatives took advantage of the disarray to oust liberal leaders from power. Military forces opposed to the government drove President Francisco Antonio Pinto and other leading officials out of the capital and defeated government military forces at the battle of Lircay.

Chile was governed by a succession of conservative presidents for the next three decades, but the most important and influential person among the conservatives never was president. Diego Portales had been the leader of the forces that had deposed the liberals and federalists in the national government. In the new government he held two important executive positions—minister of the interior and minister of war. His greatest contribution was the influence his concepts and ideas for government had upon the constitution that was adopted in 1833, which reformed Chile into what historians call the Portalian state. So enduring was this constitution that it remained Chile's official governing document until 1925.

The new constitution strongly concentrated power in the office of the president, giving that position far greater discretion than that granted to the congress. The conservatives acting under Portales's guidance reversed many of the liberals' policies, preserving full ownership rights for large landholders and restoring Catholicism to its previously privileged position. Harsh repression and enforcement measures were taken to restore civil order, but the conservatives were successful in restabilizing Chile. The government also undertook construction of new transportation and communications systems, helping to modernize Chile and improve its economy. Although electoral participation was strictly limited and the ruling powers exerted influence over the process, a long succession of Chilean leaders were democratically elected to office during the nineteenth century.

Chile also grew in military power and prestige under the conservative government. A war against a coalition between Peru and Bolivia, to the north of Chile, proved beneficial to the country. Chile undertook this war after its two northern neighbors announced they were uniting into an alliance that Chile perceived as a threat. The war lasted from 1836 to 1839, when Chile, with help from Britain, defeated the Peru-Bolivia alliance in battles on both the land and the sea. Chile subsequently emerged as a regional military power with a formidable army and navy.

The relationship Chile had with Britain, which at that time held the largest empire in the world, also benefited Chile economically. During the first few decades of independence, newly discovered deposits led to dramatic increases in silver exports, many of which went to Britain and the member nations of its commonwealth. Worldwide demand for copper also increased, and Chile had the largest copper deposits of any nation in the world. Chile's location at the southern end of South America also made its ports natural stopping points for ships bound from Europe to the west coast of North and South America. The port city of Valparaíso was a thriving shipping center, especially after Chile's military defeat of Peru and Bolivia.

PEACEFUL GOVERNMENT TRANSITION

Succeeding Chilean presidents gradually decreased the authoritarianism first imposed after the conservatives took over, and also increasingly acted to improve social services in the country. From the 1840s to the 1860s a succession of conservative presidents strengthened education in Chile, opening a national university and expanding school construction. Transportation and communication systems were also improved, with Chile becoming the first South American nation to have a national railroad. Beginning in the 1860s, Chilean governments began to be composed of members from both the liberal and conservative parties, as well as members of other, newer political parties that had taken up the causes of middle-class and urban workers. Among the progressive measures taken was the extension of voting rights to all literate adult males and eliminating property ownership requirements that had historically greatly restricted voting. Some of the Catholic Church's exclusive privileges were moderated, and greater religious tolerance was espoused, largely to accommodate new European immigrants from Protestant and Orthodox Christian countries.

In spite of these efforts, the conservative government faced opposition. Alliances between liberals and federalists mounted rebellions against the leadership in both 1851 and 1859. Over two thousand people were killed in the 1851 uprising. Beginning in the 1850s, the central government also faced renewed hostilities with the Mapuche Indians in the south. Attempts to push the Chilean frontier further south with new settlements and military encampments incited reaction from the Mapuche, who had more or less been peacefully coexisting with the Chileans for many years. Even with a larger army and a big technological advantage, Chile could not permanently subdue the Mapuche until 1881.

The most important military confrontation in Chile's history took place from 1879 to 1883. Known as the War of the Pacific, it once again pitted Chile against an alliance of Peru and Bolivia. The focus of this war was territory in the Atacama Desert that was especially rich in nitrate deposits. Nitrates were used in making fertilizers and gunpowder and were a highly valued commodity in Europe at that time. This area also had significant copper deposits. Once again Chile was victorious in the conflict, and this triumph proved to be historically significant to Chile and to South America as a whole. This is reflected in the following description of the effects and aftermath of the war, found in *Chile: A Country Study*:

> Chile acquired two northern provinces—Tarapacá from Peru and Antofagasta from Bolivia. These territories encompassed most of the Atacama Desert and blocked off Bolivia's outlet to the Pacific Ocean. The war gave Chile control over nitrate exports, which would dominate the

THE BATTLE OF IQUIQUE

Fought on May 21, 1879, the battle of Iquique is hailed as one of the great moments in Chile's history. Although the battle essentially ended in a draw between the naval forces of Peru and Chile, it came to symbolize bravery and valor among Chilean fighters, personified in naval commander Arturo Prat Chacón, who became a legend as a result of this battle.

Prat commanded one of two ships stationed in the waters off Iquique, which was at the time under Peruvian control. Prat's ship, the *Esmeralda*, and the other Chilean ship, the *Covadonga*, were both made of wood. Wooden ships were becoming outdated by that time with the building of metal combat ships, and that was vividly illustrated when two modern Peruvian battleships attacked the Chilean vessels. When it became clear that the Chilean ships could not withstand the assault, Prat provided cover for *Covadonga* to get away while he engaged the Peruvian battleship the *Huascar*. When the *Esmeralda* was on the brink of being sunk, Prat raised his sword, shouted "¡Al abordaje!" meaning, "Follow me aboard!" and signaled to his men to follow him. Prat then jumped aboard the enemy ship, which was ramming his ship in an effort to crush it. Prat and the sailors who followed him were all slain in battle and came to be recognized as national heroes in Chile for their sacrifice.

The other Chilean ship, the *Covadonga*, was able to lure the other Peruvian ship, the *Independencia*, to run aground in shallow water, but it would be another two years before Chile would emerge victorious in the war. Prat's contributions are commemorated in Chile with a monument in Valparaíso, where his remains are also interred.

national economy until the 1920s, possession of copper deposits that would eclipse nitrate exports by the 1930s, great power status along the entire Pacific Coast of South America, and an enduring symbol of patriotic pride in the person of naval hero Arturo Prat Chacón [a ship commander who lost his life in a major battle of the war].[6]

With its victory in the War of the Pacific and its gaining the Atacama territory, Chile's position as a regional economic and military power was solidified.

The 1891 Civil War

Chile's record of success for peaceful government transitions ended in 1891. By the late nineteenth century, increasing numbers of people from the new and emerging political parties were gaining seats in the congress, and they wielded this new strength to oppose presidential decisions and policies. President José Manuel Balmecada responded by trying to assert dictatorial powers and override the congress. This led to a violent confrontation between the executive and legislative branches of government, with the nation's army and navy coming down on different sides of the conflict—the army with the president, the navy with congress. After two intense battles between fellow Chileans in August 1891, Balmecada stepped down from office, appointed a war hero to be his replacement, and then killed himself while sequestered in the Argentine embassy. Congress quickly acted to assert itself more actively and prominently, and six decades of Chilean governance under dominant national presidents came to an end. It would soon become clear, however, that the power structure in Chile was still dominated by a small elite group and that the shift of power from the president to the congress would make little difference to most of the people of Chile.

3

GROWTH, PROGRESS, AND DESPAIR: A CENTURY OF CONTRAST

Social and political reform continued and accelerated in Chile during the twentieth century. Continued economic growth and rising education and literacy rates fueled even greater growth in political activity. The government increased efforts to improve the overall standard of living in Chile and extend civil and political rights, and Chile became known as a nation steeped in a progressive political tradition. However, by the 1970s the trend toward social activism and political liberalism reached the point where extreme liberal and radical political factions came to power in the central government. This provoked a reaction among the conservative opposition that resulted in the most traumatic and gruesome event and time period in Chile's history: the violent military coup of 1973, in which President Salvador Allende was killed, and the dictatorial regime of army general Augusto Pinochet.

ERA OF CONGRESSIONAL RULE

The civil war of 1891 that led to congressional supremacy in Chile did not result in a shift of the concentration of political power among the population. In fact, mostly the same people—wealthy landowners, mine owners, and other major industrialists—continued to be the primary beneficiaries of government action, and there was little improvement in the living conditions or social standing of Chile's working and poor classes. Research conducted at the beginning of the twentieth century revealed just how serious poverty and illiteracy were among large portions of the population. Increasing unionization of miners and urban workers led to strikes and violent confrontations with government forces in the late nineteenth and early twentieth centuries. A raised awareness of the hardship suffered by many Chileans led to support for social and economic reform that grew strong by the 1920s. As *The Cambridge Encyclopedia of Latin America* states, "The contrast between mass poverty and ostentatious opulence seemed to cry out for attention. The political agenda thus gradually altered in Chile."[7]

A new president dedicated to liberal reform, Arturo Alessandri, was elected to lead Chile in 1920. He narrowly won the election by directly appealing to the middle and working classes as well as intellectuals committed to reform, but he had little support among those in the government establishment. They showed their opposition by threatening to block Alessandri from taking power. His election victory had been very narrow and needed ratification by the congress to be finalized. Massive demonstrations by Alessandri's supporters convinced his opponents not to obstruct him, but the opposition continued to work against him. The congress consistently opposed his reforms, and a group of military leaders removed him from office in late 1924. However, political progressivism had grown in Chile to the point where

Poverty was a serious problem in Chile at the turn of the twentieth century. Pictured is a hillside slum in Valparaíso in the early 1900s.

many in the military, especially among the younger officers, were themselves liberals and reformists, and another, pro-Alessandri military faction quickly restored him to power in early 1925.

THE 1925 CONSTITUTION

Once restored to power, Alessandri drafted Chile's first new constitution since the Portalian constitution of 1833. It was approved in a national vote in 1925, and it represented a major broadening of rights and protections for Chile's people. Workers' rights to organize were recognized, the social welfare of all citizens was provided for, and greater representation for all political parties in legislative elections was established. New powers were given to the president to counter the overriding influence of the congress, but presidents were limited to just one successive term, which was extended from five to six years.

Chile experienced a brief period of instability after Alessandri left office. Carlos Ibáñez, president from 1927 to 1931, created a national police force and imposed authoritarian control until he was pressured out of office in July 1931. Stability was not restored until Alessandri was returned to power in an election in 1932. He effectively enforced the new constitution, and Chile was governed civilly and democratically for the next forty years, reassuming the status of a stable and progressive nation despite a trend toward dictatorships and military regimes among other Latin American nations during that time.

Among the rights extended was the end of the official designation of the Catholic Church as the state religion and the recognition of equal rights for all religions. Also, women, who had not yet benefited from the nation's broadening of voting rights, achieved this right in 1949. Economic conditions also generally improved. The wealth provided by Chile's nitrate deposits declined sharply as artificial substitutes were invented that could be produced and purchased less expensively came to dominate the market. However, Chile's copper exports continued to grow and provide substantial revenues. Increased exportation of crops, wines, and livestock products also produced ongoing economic growth in Chile, although the nation did suffer setbacks during times of global economic hardship, such as the Great Depression of the 1930s.

ARTURO ALESSANDRI

First elected president in 1920, Arturo Alessandri served a total of twelve years as Chile's head of state, the longest any elected leader of the nation has ever served. Alessandri gained power by appealing to the many laborers and middle-class Chileans who had entered into Chile's political process by the 1920s. Alessandri's economic programs won him support among the lower and middle classes, but his personal charm and dynamism were also a major part of his appeal. Simon Collier and William F. Slater elaborate on this in *A History of Chile, 1808–1994:*

> His rhetorical gifts were considerable: no other Chilean politician of the twentieth century has equaled him in this respect. He was the nearest any modern Chilean politician has ever come . . . to being a "charismatic leader." The magic of his name was sufficient, nearly forty years later, to help one of his sons win the Chilean presidency. Stories about his speechmaking abound. He could hold a crowd as few others have been able to do.

As president, Arturo Allesandri favored a program of social reform to benefit the middle class and poor.

Chile's activist progressive government supported industrialization efforts and underwrote new and emerging businesses to further bolster the national economy.

THE CHILE–U.S. RELATIONSHIP

One important development during the twentieth century, especially the years following World War II, was the growth of trade and diplomatic relations with the United States, which came to replace Britain as Chile's most important ally and economic partner. This relationship brought benefits as well as consequences.

The United States provided military and economic aid to Chile in expectation of Chile's support in the U.S.–Soviet Union Cold War. One form of economic aid was credit extended to the government to help it pay for its social and national industrial programs. These programs became so large and expensive that Chile became dependent upon large foreign loans to maintain them. Growing debt to other nations led to high inflation, or rising costs of consumer goods, which put a strain on the finances of most Chileans. At the same time economic growth stagnated in Chile, making it difficult for wages and incomes to keep pace with the rising prices. Opposition politicians became more vocal and strident as economic conditions worsened, and some Chileans became concerned or dissatisfied with the U.S.–Chile relationship, fearing Chile was being hurt by being overly dependent on the United States.

One action taken by President Gabriel González Videla in 1948 was widely attributed to Chile's relationship with the United States. The political pluralism and tolerance that had come to be a hallmark of Chile suffered a setback when Videla outlawed the Communist Party, which had grown considerably and become highly visible in Chile and throughout Latin America since the early twentieth century. Videla also cut off relations with several enemy nations of the United States, including its major rival the Soviet Union. Cold War politics would continue to play an important role in Chile's destiny during the mid- to late twentieth century, having a profound impact on Chile's politics and, ultimately, upon everyday life in the country.

THE SHIFTING ROLE OF THE CHURCH

Another major shift affecting Chile that occurred in the twentieth century was in the role played by the Catholic Church in society. Throughout its early history the church had been aligned with conservative political forces and had been a great beneficiary of Chile's traditional power elite. Advocacy for social reform and the improvement of living conditions for the poor had not been a major part of the church's activity during Chile's history. The global conflict between communism and the Western powers made the Chilean Catholic Church even less inclined to embrace social reform, as such movements came to be associated with worldwide communism, which the Catholic leadership abhorred. However, beginning in the 1930s Catholic leaders associated with the conservative party began branching out and establishing their own political organizations. These spin-off Christian parties advocated moderate social reform while rejecting radicalism, and also called for the preservation of civil rule and democratic politics. Two of these parties joined forces in the 1950s to form a new party, the Christian Democrats.

This new party rapidly gained a large and devoted following, and immediately played an important role in Chile's political scene. History professors Simon Collier and William F. Slater, coauthors of *A History of Chile, 1808–1994*, explained the Christian Democrats' wide and powerful appeal, claiming they "embodied a serious attachment to social reform . . . combined with a fierce attachment to democracy—in short, a 'revolution in liberty.'"[8] In fact, in 1958, just one year after the formation of the party, its presidential candidate, Eduardo Frei, finished a strong third with over 20 percent of the vote. Membership in the Christian Democratic Party rose enormously over the next six years, when the next presidential election took place. This time Frei won with over 56 percent of the vote, the largest total any candidate for president had ever received in Chile. Two years later Christian Democrats scored another solid victory in legislative elections, winning a majority of seats in the lower house, the Chamber of Deputies, and substantially increasing their presence in the senate. Many Chileans identified with and admired the Christian Democrat call for moderate social reform and improvement in living conditions for the poor without resorting to a radical government system such as communism.

However, once in power, Frei and his fellow party members in congress had to contend with increasingly hardened opposition from both conservatives and liberals. The Christian Democrats had been the first to carry out meaningful agricultural land reform to benefit rural peasants, angering the powerful landowners. They also made it even easier for urban and industrial workers to organize, and undertook a

THE CATHOLIC CHURCH IN CHILE

The Catholic Church enjoyed the status of being the official religion of Chile for nearly one hundred years. Conservatives in government preserved the Catholic Church's privileged position, and a close relationship formed between the church and the leadership of the Conservative Party. The church's leadership was not active in the socially progressive efforts and political movements undertaken during the nineteenth and early twentieth centuries, as the interests of the lower economic classes were seen as contradictory to those of the church's allies in government.

However, in the twentieth century prominent church members began to participate in efforts to help the poor and improve economic and social conditions in Chile. Four Catholic members of the Conservative Party, including future president Eduardo Frei, broke away and began their own political party, the Falange, in 1939. While seeking to maintain the church's influence in society, they also advocated programs to help the disadvantaged. The Falange joined other Christian political parties to form the highly successful Christian Democratic Party in 1957.

Reforms implemented by the Catholic Church leadership at the Vatican in the 1960s led to activism on the part of Chile's church leadership itself. The church took a prominent role in the social programs implemented by Frei and the Christian Democratic government. Under Pinochet's dictatorship the church became the only viable source of political opposition within the country. Even when church leaders spoke out strongly against government actions, the military leaders did not react—many of them, including Pinochet himself, were practicing and devout Catholics. This led people who were persecuted by the government to seek protection from the church. In *Culture and Customs of Chile*, Guillermo Castillo-Feliú says that as a result of the changes it underwent during the twentieth century, "the Roman Catholic Church in Chile has become . . . more representative of Chilean society as a whole, no longer allying itself only with conservative elements."

massive expansion of schools. Frei's government strengthened the copper industry and increased the proportion of copper mines over which Chile claimed ownership and exclusive rights. Yet for the Communists and other hard-line leftists, these actions were insufficient. The liberal opposition called for more sweeping and complete reforms, and resented what they considered the encroachment upon their natural base of support among laborers and the rural poor by the Christian Democrats. Hence, the most radical reformers, as well as the decidedly conservative landowners, became adamantly opposed to the Christian Democrats.

THE RISE OF THE LEFT

With the extension of voting rights ongoing throughout Chile's history, the new and emerging political parties that arose had a large body of people to recruit from. As the new entrants into the electoral process were usually poorer and of a lower social class, it was natural that the new parties would be more liberal and progressive than the existing parties, who were made up of the wealthy elite. The radical party, first formed during the nineteenth century, was the largest and most powerful of these new parties for many years. In the twentieth century newer political parties based on the concepts of nineteenth-century theorist Karl Marx took positions even more liberal than those of the radicals, advocating full government takeovers of industries and farmlands, and worker and peasant takeovers of the businesses where they labored. The Communist and Socialist parties of Chile emerged in 1912 and 1933 respectively, and although they did not grow as large as the conservatives, liberals, or radicals, they did become significant forces on Chile's open and increasingly varied political scene in the early- to midtwentieth century. Miners and urban laborers especially were drawn to these new leftist parties.

Salvador Allende, a self-proclaimed Marxist, celebrates his victory in the 1970 presidential election.

One of the short-lived governments that presided over Chile in the early 1930s was actually a Socialist regime. It took control by military coup and was quickly displaced. However, a coalition of radical, Communist, and Socialist parties combined forces to elect a president, Aguirre Cedra, who won just over 50 percent of the vote in 1938. Cedra had been a member of the more moderate radical party, but in 1958 another candidate ran for election. Backed by a liberal alliance, Salvador Allende was a self-proclaimed Marxist who openly advocated property ownership transfers to workers and the full nationalization of major Chilean industries. Allende came close to being elected, losing by less than 3 percent. The winner, backed by the older conservative and liberal parties, was Jorge Alessandri, son of earlier president Arturo Alessandri. After Frei's Christian Democratic presidency in the 1960s, the election of 1970 presented a sharply fragmented electorate between hard leftists and rightists and the centrists who were now led by the Christian Democrats. Once again a candidate of the liberal coalition, Allende this time won with about 36 percent of the vote, beating Alessandri, who had narrowly beaten him last time by about 1 percent. This would prove to be the start of a momentous chain of events in Chile's history.

SOCIALIST CHILE

Chileans were so concerned about having elected a Marxist president that the congress demanded that Allende sign a document guaranteeing he would preserve democratic and political freedoms after taking office. This demand was in response to widespread suspicion that Allende would, like Marxist leaders in other nations, impose a totalitarian government upon the country once he was in power. Allende did not attack the political opposition or eliminate free speech or press rights, but he did take measures toward redistributing wealth and power in Chile that went far beyond what any government had done before. This caused a convulsive reaction from conservative political factions and the controlling elites who suffered large-scale loss of property and personal profit under Allende's regime.

The privileged class experienced these losses when Allende fully nationalized mining and other important industries, banks, and large agricultural estates. Ownership of

SALVADORE ALLENDE AND AUGUSTO PINOCHET

The two principals who clashed in 1973 over control of Chile's government held drastically different ideas and opinions regarding government. Having been a medical doctor and an early adherent to socialism, Allende entered politics in the 1930s, winning election to the senate and serving in a presidential cabinet before beginning a series of four runs for the presidency of Chile in 1952. Allende was finally elected the fourth time, although he only received 36 percent of the vote in that election.

Augusto Pinochet entered a military academy at age sixteen and was a career army officer following graduation. He came to dislike civilian government when elected leaders dramatically cut Chile's defense budgets during the 1960s. He also came to dislike leftist political organizations when he led military forces against coal miners whose unions were associated with the Communist Party. Nevertheless, Allende actually saw fit to appoint Pinochet to important jobs, such as commanding the Santiago army garrison and later to the position of chief of the army general staff. While giving the appearance of supporting the civilian government of Allende in his official capacity, Pinochet, according to a book about the coup published later, had contempt for Allende well before he took power from him. In *A Nation of Enemies: Chile Under Pinochet*, journalist Pamela Constable and Latin American studies professor Arturo Valenzuela quote Pinochet as saying, "With great bitterness we men of arms watched the road Chile had taken, and we felt the desperation of impotence. As a soldier sworn to protect the fatherland, I felt inhibited from acting, because the institution of chaos was the very government . . . to which I owed obedience."

many factories was turned over to the workers, and the farmlands to the resident peasant laborers. In some cases militant workers seized control of estates or businesses themselves, without government authority or supervision. Allende also raised pay for lower- and middle-class workers while freezing market prices. This gave most Chileans much strong buying power initially, but later caused problems as hyped demand created shortages of many products and led to more serious inflation—the worst Chile had ever experienced. This put a strain on the national economy that was made worse by the ending of credit and economic aid from the United States, which was displeased over the seizure of American property during Allende's nationalization of business and industry.

The United States also disapproved of Allende's Socialist economic policies and disliked his resuming of diplomatic relations with pro-Soviet Communist countries such as Cuba and North Vietnam. Without economic assistance from the United States, the Chilean government suffered shortages in funds. Chile's congress was controlled by conservatives and moderates who regarded Allende as too extreme. They also worked against Allende, trying to prevent his initiatives from becoming enacted, although Allende used emergency legislation passed in the 1930s to bypass the legislature and implement some of them nevertheless.

By 1973 animosity between Allende's government and its supporters and their opposition had grown severe. Both sides hoped legislative elections that year would help shift the balance of power in their favor, but instead election results were indecisive, with conservatives and moderates winning about 55 percent of the seats but the leftist alliance nevertheless gaining additional seats above what it had held before. With both sides emboldened, demonstrators took to the streets and violence ensued. Increasingly Allende's opponents looked to the military to bring an end to his regime. When opponents in the congress accused him of violating the constitution and abusing his presidential power, military forces acted against Allende.

CARNAGE AND TYRANNY

The military attack that took place against President Allende on September 11, 1973, was well planned and tactically executed. Heads of the various armed forces were involved, and they brought a tumultuous assault upon the presidential palace. Army troops surrounded the palace and fired upon it while air force planes dropped bombs from above. Allende was dead by the end of the day—later evidence seems to indicate that he took his own life—and a military government took over that would rule Chile with uncharacteristic authoritarianism for the next sixteen years.

The head of the army, General Augusto Pinochet, took control of the country under the new government. He immediately took extreme measures such as imposing a national curfew, disbanding congress, outlawing opposition political parties, closing down press and media opposed to the military government, and arresting and murdering or torturing those known to have been or suspected of being connected with the Allende government. In a particularly dramatic event, thousands of people from a variety of backgrounds, most notably politically oriented musicians, artists, writers, and activists, were herded into a soccer stadium by government forces, and many of them were never heard from again. People who were taken by the government during this period in this manner who failed to return afterward came to be known as The Disappeared. These abductions and other inhumane behaviors became the focus of major international human rights efforts, and Chilean activists who were able to leave the country to avoid being seized by the new government were vigilant in speaking out against these actions.

Along with reversing Chile's trend toward liberalism and political pluralism, the Pinochet government also implemented dramatically different economic policies. Government spending was sharply curtailed, property rights of the elite were restored, and most of the nationalization that had taken place under Allende's brief regime was also negated. Instead, Chile was laid open to foreign investors like never before. A team of U.S. economists, who became known as

A Chilean soldier stands guard over political prisoners in a Santiago stadium after Pinochet ousted Allende in 1973.

the Chicago Boys because of their study at the University of Chicago School of Economics, guided the Chilean government in an economic reformation that succeeded in slowing inflation and closing government budget deficits. While international observers and human rights activists spoke out against the Chilean regime, major Western nations nevertheless continued to trade extensively with Chile and provide support and assistance. The United States in particular regarded Chile as strategic in its struggle with the Soviet Union, and considered the Pinochet regime far preferable to the one that had preceded it. Nevertheless, Western governments did urge Pinochet to ease repressive measures and restore democratic freedoms. The Catholic Church also called for the restoration of democratic government and basic civil

General Augusto Pinochet, who ruled Chile until 1990, reviews his troops inside the presidential palace in Santiago.

rights, as well as for some resumption of economic assistance for the poor of the nation, whose situation had declined severely in the wake of the strict budget austerity measures that had been taken in the 1970s.

Pressure upon the military government mounted when the country was struck by an economic downturn in the early 1980s. This was a period of worldwide recession, and Chile was once again beset by stagnant growth and spiraling inflation. Need for foreign support required Chile to accommodate those demanding that it restore democratic control of the government.

A constitution was passed in a tightly controlled national election in 1980 that kept Pinochet in power until 1990. Another election was slated for 1988, but this time the government conducted the election openly, yielding to international and domestic pressure. Pinochet's name was the only one on the ballot, but voters had the option of deciding whether he should remain in power or step down. The result was 45 percent for Pinochet and 55 percent against him. Although surprised and dismayed by the results, Pinochet abided by the election. He left power and free elections were held the following year. Since then Chile has returned to and maintained its long-held tradition of having regular elections with a wide variety of active and influential political parties, and being governed by democratically chosen leaders.

PINOCHET'S CONTINUING IMPACT

The 1981 constitution assured Pinochet a seat in the Chilean Senate and the position of commander in chief of the armed forces for the duration of his life. Along with other members of the military government who also were given permanent unelected seats in the government, Pinochet prevented effective investigations and prosecutions of crimes and human rights violations that occurred during his regime. Many Chileans were frustrated and anguished that they could not be fully rid of Pinochet. Those who had suffered personal loss or persecution under his regime felt they were denied satisfaction and justice.

Some hope that legal action could be taken against Pinochet arose in 1998 when legal authorities responding to an arrest warrant issued by a Spanish judge detained him on a visit to London. The warrant claimed Pinochet had committed human rights violations against Spanish citizens in Chile and needed to stand trial for his crimes. The British government deliberated on whether to send Pinochet to Spain but ultimately decided not to, based on the grounds that he was too unhealthy to stand trial, and Pinochet returned to Chile. Although he was stripped of immunity from prosecution when he resigned his government posts in Chile in 1998, Chilean courts have similarly held that Pinochet is unfit for trial. Even with democracy and civil order restored, the legacy of Pinochet continues to weigh heavily upon Chile, leaving many with questions and grievances unresolved.

CHILE'S PEOPLE AND THEIR LIFESTYLES

4

Chileans are remarkably unified ethnically and culturally, with a national heritage and religion shared among a vast majority of the people. Even with the large and greatly diverse territory Chile covers, daily life is very much alike for most Chileans throughout the country. However, Chileans engage in a great diversity of occupations, businesses, recreations, and spiritual activities, and although their culture may be predominantly influenced by Spanish and Indian cultures, all the peoples that have come to Chile have had an impact on everyday life there.

ETHNICITY AND RELIGION

Two cultural features of Chile unite huge majorities of its population: mixed Spanish and Indian ancestry, and membership in the Catholic Church. Over 90 percent of the population is of mixed heritage; only about 2 to 3 percent each are wholly European or Indian. People of African or Asian descent make up an even smaller portion of the population. The major remaining Indians are the Mapuche in the South, the Aymarás in the North, and the Rapi Nui of Easter Island. Most of the wholly European Chileans originated in such places as Germany, Italy, Wales, and the Balkans. These groups came in migrations during the nineteenth and early twentieth centuries.

Among the later immigrant groups and the Indian population there is some continued general use of native languages at home. The Araucanian language of the Mapuche can be heard in the markets of Temuco, and in some places newspapers and other publications are published in languages other than Spanish. In the towns of Valdivia and Puerto Montt, where large numbers of Germans settled and remain, one can even see signs and advertisements printed

Churchgoers crowd around the pulpit of the Church of Saint Teresa of the Andes during Sunday mass.

in German. However, the official language of Chile is Spanish, and it is the one that is used for almost all spoken and written communication.

As with language, there is an overwhelming imbalance of religious diversity. Judaism, Protestantism, Orthodox Christianity, Islam, and Buddhism have all been brought to Chile, and some Indians continue to practice their ancient religions. Yet nearly 80 percent of Chileans are Roman Catholics, although the level of active church participation varies greatly. Still, church practices and ceremonies constitute important parts of Chilean life. Most children undergo baptism in a Catholic church, and First Communion and Holy Confirmation are major events in a child's life. Most marriages are also church affairs.

HOLIDAYS AND FESTIVITIES

Some of Chile's largest and most important festivals and holidays are rooted in religious tradition. The entire weekend of Easter, including Good Friday and Holy Saturday in addition to Easter Sunday, are officially designated holidays. On the Sunday after Easter, villages in much of the country celebrate the religious festival known as Domingo de Cuasimodo. Residents dress in brightly colored costumes and carry Christian pennants and signs. Floats and houses are also vibrantly decorated, and horsemen dress in special attire resembling that of knights from the Middle Ages, all to celebrate the resurrection of Christ. Priests ride in carriages surrounded by the pageantry, administering Holy Communion to people along the way.

Christmas is also celebrated with great fanfare. Because Chile is in the Southern Hemisphere, Christmas coincides with the beginning of summer, and many Christmas festivities are held outdoors. The central religious event for Chileans at Christmas is a midnight mass called *miso de gallo* (the cock's mass). It is customary for Chileans to follow the mass with an outdoor feast that lasts several hours. Although roast beef and turkey may be common fare for Christmas dinner in North America, Chileans prefer seafood. One very popular dish, *curanto*, is cooked outdoors, in sandpits along the beach. It is prepared with a combination of seafood, pork, chicken, eggs, vegetables, and herbs and spices. Although it is very late when Chileans return home after these festivities, they usually stay up to exchange gifts with close friends and family members. Christmas Day tends to be quiet, with people gathering in their homes with their families. Many Chileans begin holiday trips to the beach immediately following Christmas. Throughout Chile, New Year's Eve is celebrated boisterously, much like it is in the rest of the world, with revelers staying up past midnight eating, drinking, and dancing.

Other major religious holidays are the Feast of Saints Peter and Paul at the end of June, the Assumption of the Virgin Mary on August 15, All Saints' Day on November 1, and the Immaculate Conception on December 8. Some of the most splendorous festivals, or fiestas, are held in honor of regional patron saints. The nation's patron mother, the Virgin of Carmel, is celebrated in a festival held at the village of La Tirana each year in July. Featuring dance troupes and musicians in highly synchronized and rhythmic performances, the festival represents a blend of European and American Indian styles. The festival lasts a week, with the music and dance continuing nonstop. Individuals perform for as many as three straight days, pausing only briefly for food and costume changes. People gather from around Chile for prolonged sessions of prayer, meditation, sermons, and singing.

Chileans also celebrate several holidays that commemorate major events in their national history or honor people's contributions. Like much of the world, Chile celebrates Labor Day on May 1. May 21 is Navy Day, in honor of those who fought in the naval battle of Iquique in the War of the Pacific in 1879. A large and impressive monument to the battle stands in the city of Valparaíso. No fewer than three national holidays take place in September. The anniversary of the military coup of 1973 is commemorated on September 11. Although that is generally a somber occasion, Chileans enjoy celebrating their nation's independence day, September 18. Dining, dancing, and drinking are commonplace through-

During the festival known as Domingo de Cuasimodo, a Chilean man prepares to ride his bike decorated with a poster venerating Jesus.

CHILEANS' SENSE OF TIME

When attending a social occasion at someone's home, Chileans consider it polite to arrive at least fifteen to thirty minutes late. The larger and grander the event, the later the guests are expected to arrive. Showing up promptly or early is considered presumptuous and selfish, implying that the guest is overanxious and expects too much of the host or hostess. Foreigners who attend social gatherings and arrive at the designated time or earlier are sometimes surprised to find that their hosts have not yet completed preparations.

However, Chileans have a very different attitude regarding timeliness and punctuality for business and professional meetings. Being on time for meetings is considered imperative, especially when meeting new or unfamiliar people. This is because Chileans consider it essential to take time to get to know a person well before establishing a business relationship.

out the country, and many places hold large outdoor public parties. The following day Chileans continue their patriotic celebration on Armed Forces Day. The main celebratory event is a military parade along the major streets of Santiago. In October, Columbus Day is regarded with mixed feelings in Chile. Negative feelings about Columbus have become widespread because of his mistreatment of indigenous peoples and the Spanish conquest and subjugation of the Indians that followed his arrival. In recent years Chileans and others in South America have used the occasion to celebrate their common heritage with Spain, rather than to honor or commemorate Columbus.

Besides holiday celebrations, Chileans find other ways to have fun. Beaches can be found all along the country's extensive shoreline, and during the summer months people flock to them in droves. Besides swimming, many people also enjoy scuba diving, snorkeling, and boating. Likewise, skiing is a very popular sport in winter, and the Andes Mountains provide many opportunities for pursuing this pastime. The largest ski area in Latin America, consisting of four resorts, is located just east of Santiago. Valle Nevado, La Parva, El Colorado, and Farellones feature a variety of slopes from beginner level to advanced. Both deep-sea and lake fishing are widely enjoyed among Chileans.

A Chilean family relaxes on the grass of a Santiago park. Social life in Chile revolves primarily around the family.

FAMILY LIFE

Many Chileans enjoy large festivals and lively outdoor activities; so too do they enjoy quiet games of cards, chess, and dominoes at home with family members. Backyard picnics and barbecues abound in Chile during warm weather season, when extended families and close friends gather frequently on weekends and holidays. Most Chileans' social lives are closely entwined with their families, and many young Chileans meet their future spouses through friends of their parents or other close relatives. It is also common for grown children to remain home with their parents until they get married, and then continue to live nearby and visit frequently. Most Chileans marry and begin families in their early-to-mid-twenties.

Gender roles in Chile tend to follow the same lines as in most of Latin America. Men are considered the heads of families, responsible for providing a living income, while women are expected to care for the home and children. However, women make up about 35 percent of the Chilean workforce, and their representation in some occupations is noteworthy. About half of all Chilean dentists are women. The number of women judges, at least at the local level, is also large, and women's representation in the field of journalism is about the same as men's. Most upper-class women, and some middle-class women, have maids that help them with their shopping, cooking, and other domestic chores.

FOOD AND DRINK

To a great extent daily family life centers on meals, which are usually eaten together with immediate family members. Chileans tend to eat little for breakfast, usually just toast and jam with coffee. Lunch is generally the most substantial meal during the day. It is eaten in the early to midafternoon, and lunch breaks from jobs tend to be long. The lunches themselves consist of multiple courses, with soups or appetizers to start, a main course of meat and vegetables, and sweets or fruit for dessert. At one time companies commonly allowed their employees more than two hours off in the middle of the day to return home for a siesta—a large meal and a nap or rest—before returning to work. This practice is uncommon now, especially in the large cities, where increased traffic and commute times make siestas impractical. But Chileans still enjoy lingering over a meal and talking with each other, whether in restaurants or at home. As Castillo-Feliú discusses in *Culture and Customs of Chile:*

> Chileans, like other Latin Americans and Spaniards, like to enjoy a leisurely meal, whenever this is possible, where food is consumed in the company of good friends or family, and where time enjoyed after the meal is over (a *sobremesa*, sitting at the table after the meal) is an important experience. It is one cultural tradition that Chileans would be loath to abandon even if it seems to clash with the pace of modern life.[9]

Dinner or supper comes late in the evening, often as late as nine o'clock. It is usually simpler with smaller portions than lunch, although similar kinds of foods are often served, and there may be more than one course as well. Children are often fed a late afternoon or evening snack, and Chileans have a meal they call *el té* that is much like the meal of tea in

Britain, usually consisting only of bread, cakes, or light fare, along with tea or coffee to drink.

Chilean cuisine is influenced both by Spanish and other European cuisine and by native American crops and Indian recipes. The immense geographic diversity of Chile has also provided a great variety of foods from the land, lakes, and sea. Chilean dishes are among the most intriguing and eclectic of any country's. The food most emblematic of Chile is the empanada (Spanish for "turnover"). Empanadas consist of thick pastry crust filled with mixtures of ingredients such as meat, fish, cheese, eggs, herbs, or fruits (for dessert empanadas). Empanadas are often deep-fried and eaten as snacks, but Chileans are especially fond of baked empanadas. These are usually larger than the fried sort and can be eaten as a meal by themselves. An especially scrumptious empanada contains cubed or ground beef, chopped onions, raisins, hard-boiled eggs, olive oil, red and black pepper, cumin, and water.

Other Chilean dishes make use of the local crops and creatures, such as *porotos granados*, a stew made from corn, squash, onions, garlic, and either cranberry or navy beans. *Congrio*, or conger eel, is caught in Chile's coastal waters and is designated a national dish. *Congrio* can be served grilled, baked, fried, or stewed with tomatoes, onions, and potatoes. Sea urchins are another Chilean delicacy. Some Chileans eat live urchins picked fresh from the sea, garnished with lemon juice.

Chileans are also dessert lovers, and many shops stock assortments of cakes, pastries, and confections. Many Chileans also prepare these at home. A common ingredient in Chilean desserts is *manjar*, also called *dulce de leche*, or sweet milk. *Manjar* is made by combining milk and sugar and slow cooking the mixture until it turns brown and thickens. Besides being used as a filling for cakes and pastries, *manjar* is also dried and sold as fudgelike candy.

Coffee or tea is often drunk with sweets in Chile, but coffee is usually instant. Those seeking stronger coffee can order *cafecito*, or espresso. Instead of coffee or regular tea, some Chileans prefer another hot caffeinated beverage, an herbal tea called yerba maté. Originally drunk by the Indians, yerba maté is now popular in much of Chile. The tea is made by grinding leaves from a holly berry shrub and blending them with hot water. It requires a special drinking straw called a *bombilla*, which is designed to filter sediment from the tea. People drinking yerba maté together share the same *bombilla*. The tea is potent, and people usually drink only a little at a time.

Chilean wines enjoy global renown, and they are especially inexpensive in Chile. Popular varietals such as cabernet sauvignon and chardonnay are produced in large quantities. Malbec is another variety of red wine that is particularly good in Chile, and Chilean sauvignon blancs are fine examples of white wines. Another type of alcoholic beverage unique to the region is a liqueur called *pisco*, which is made from muscatel wine grapes. It is often drunk in a *pisco* sour, mixed with lemon juice, ice, and sugar, or in a cocktail with cola, ginger ale, or mineral water.

JOBS AND ECONOMIC STATUS

Chilean wines are a source of national pride, and for those involved in growing grapes or in import-export businesses, a means of earning a living. Still, the kinds of businesses Chileans are most likely to find themselves in are service industries,

A bakery in Santiago sells empanadas, a type of turnover stuffed with either sweet or savory fillings.

A worker empties his basket of harvested grapes in a vineyard near Santiago. Chilean wines are popular throughout the world.

manufacturing, agriculture, forestry, and fishing. Chile also has significant numbers of communication, transportation, and government workers. Although mining is a major source of revenue for Chile, only a small percentage of the population works in mining.

What Chileans do for a living, what kind of house and neighborhood they live in, and what their daily routines are like are all affected by their economic and social status and, to some extent, the region of the country in which they live. Wide disparities still exist between Chile's small number of very wealthy people and the large number who linger in poverty or work strenuously to survive, in spite of the social and economic progress that has been made in Chile throughout its history.

Over half the people in Chile live in the Central Valley, with the largest number by far living in Santiago and its suburbs. Many of the nation's wealthiest people, mostly large landowners or major industrialists, own town houses or live in high-rise luxury apartments in the central city. These people are also likely to own one or more other homes, either in the farm areas or one of the country's popular resorts. Bankers, doctors, lawyers, and senior government officials are major components of Chile's upper middle class. Their families also usually live in comfortable, relatively luxurious homes. Most government, professional, and clerical workers are part of the broader middle class that also includes union-ized industrial workers, merchants, and small business op-erators throughout the country. Their homes are usually more modest but still hospitable. Both upper- and middle-class Chileans can afford to patronize well-stocked, upscale stores and restaurants. Increasingly the area surrounding Santiago has been looking more like suburban America, complete with supermarkets, shopping malls, and modern housing developments.

Living conditions are starkly different for Santiago's poor-est inhabitants. Through most of Chile's history rural dwellers have steadily migrated to the city. Those who came to Santiago hoped to find higher-paying work than they could find in the country, where often, especially in tough economic times, no work was available. This large influx of people led to the sprouting of the dilapidated housing and shantytowns called *poblaciones callampas* around the pe-riphery of Santiago. During the late twentieth century the Chilean government made efforts to eliminate these settle-ments, or at least improve conditions by providing electric-ity and running water. Substantial new building of low-cost housing in the city was undertaken, and many poor residents of the city were relocated. Although the new housing is a marked improvement over the *poblaciones*, those who live there still suffer from overcrowding and high crime rates.

In the agricultural areas, most farm workers do not enjoy the same standard of living as their urban counterparts. They do hard physical labor for long hours every day and do not have many of the amenities and conveniences found in San-tiago. Houses are usually small, some consisting of only one room. In the northern desert regions many houses are made from adobe, but in the south, where there are dense forests, wooden homes are the norm. Along the shoreline, especially in the Archipelago, houses are often built on stilts, right alongside the water. Mining and manufacturing are major sources of employment in the north, and foresting, herding, and farm fishing are economically important in the south. Fishing and cargo shipping are major industries all along the coast. Crude oil and natural gas deposits discovered after World War II have led to energy production becoming the most important component of the economy in Tierra del Fuego.

EDUCATION

Business and industry in Chile have a well-educated populace to draw on as a workforce. The nation has always been committed to public education, and it has been a big part of Chile's success as a nation. Chilean children must attend school for eight years, and participation in the education system is nearly universal. Chile boasts a literacy rate of over 90 percent, one of the best in South America. This has come about largely because of educational improvements and reforms that were carried out by the Christian Democrats in the 1960s. Thousands of new schools were built throughout the country, making it easier for rural and remote residents to reach a school. Textbooks and teaching materials were overhauled and updated, further improving Chile's educational system.

Chilean students pose for a photo at a Santiago elementary school. Primary schooling is compulsory in Chile.

Following primary school, most Chilean youth attend secondary or vocational schools. Secondary schools are for those preparing for university studies, and vocational

CHILEAN NEWSPAPERS AND MAGAZINES

The high literacy rate in Chile means that the country produces a large number of magazines and newspapers. The daily paper *El Mercurio*, published in Santiago, is the country's most prestigious newspaper. Another paper called *El Mercurio de Valparaíso* has been published continually in that city since 1827. It is regarded as the oldest continuously published Spanish-language newspaper in the world. Most large cities have their own daily paper, and Santiago boasts at least six other daily news publications besides *El Mercurio*. A major German language weekly, *El Condor*, has been published steadily for over sixty years. *El Condor* is popular among the country's German Chilean community.

Among the most widely read magazines in Chile, *Ercilla*, published biweekly, is similar to the U.S. publications *Time* and *Newsweek*, covering an assortment of news, entertainment, and cultural topics. Although *Ercilla* is seen as conventional and reliable, a newer and edgier magazine, *Qué Pasa*, has made a name for itself by often taking controversial stands on issues and challenging authority and tradition.

schools serve those directly entering the workforce. Chile's higher education system is also of outstanding quality, and the nation has shown a strong commitment to its universities. The University of Chile was established in Santiago in 1842, replacing the colonial University of San Felipe, which had opened more than one hundred years before. The Catholic University, also in Santiago, is another major university as well as the nation's largest private university. Other large public universities are found in most of Chile's major cities, and there are a growing number of private universities as well, reflecting an ongoing desire on the part of Chileans for knowledge and learning.

5

CULTURE, THE ARTS, AND ENTERTAINMENT

For a country with a relatively small population, Chile has an impressive record of artistic and cultural achievement in a variety of creative fields. While leading Chilean artistic, literary, and musical figures have had success following traditional and classic European styles, the folk art and culture that have developed within Chile have also contributed greatly to the nation's cultural heritage. Social and political conditions have often influenced Chile's music, art, and literature. The authoritarian rule of the Pinochet regime has had an especially strong impact upon Chilean art and culture, inspiring works that have protested against and expressed powerful emotional reactions to the policies and actions of that regime.

FINE AND VISUAL ARTS

Spanish settlers in Chile imported quality works of art from Europe, particularly religious art. Many of these artifacts can still be found in Chile's churches and cathedrals. Early in Chile's history, prominent painters came from other nations and worked in Chile, among them Jose Gil de Castro of Peru and Raimundo Monvoisin of France. Both of these artists painted in a conventional method, creating mainly portraits and landscapes. The Chilean Academy of Painting, established in 1849, has helped foster fine painting. The twentieth-century painter Roberto Matta was born in Chile but also worked in Europe and the United States. Matta is a world-renowned modern artist who employs abstract and surrealistic techniques in most of his work.

Sculpture has also been prominent in Chile's culture. A sculpture called *United in Glory and Death* by nineteenth-century artist Rebeca Matte that stands outside the Museum of Fine Arts in Santiago is recognized as a leading masterpiece. Matte, who is of Chilean origin but spent most of her life abroad, also created other major works in Chile, including the battle monument in Concepción. In the twentieth century, Chilean sculptor Marta Colvin has gained international fame, exhibiting her work in leading cities throughout the world as well as in Chile.

Folk arts and crafts are a major part of Chile's artistic heritage. The Mapuche are skilled and revered crafters of jewelry, textiles and woolen goods, baskets, utensils, and animal figurines. These creations are sold in abundance in the marketplaces of Temuco and other towns in the south of Chile. Colorfully dyed woolen goods and painted boat models are specialties on the island of Chiloé. Courses dedicated specifically to Indian arts at Temuco University indicate how seriously they are regarded by Chileans.

One form of folk art that has come to have powerful significance in Chile is the *arpillera*, a wall hanging created

Rebeca Matte's sculpture United in Glory and Death *adorns the entrance to Santiago's Museum of Fine Arts.*

from patches of burlap or other sackcloth. This is a traditional folk art form in much of Latin America, but Chilean *arpilleras* gained special meaning during the most tyrannical years of the Pinochet regime. Women whose husbands, sons, fathers, and brothers had been killed or exiled or had disappeared gathered to create *arpilleras* that protested the regime's policies and drew attention to the plights of the persecuted in Chile. One especially poignant work depicted a woman dancing a courtship dance by herself. These *arpilleras* were used in protest demonstrations and, after the government began to ease restrictions, were publicly exhibited and used in theatrical productions. High-quality *arpilleras* with more general themes continue to be produced in Chile. The village of Isla Negra, along the Pacific coast, is well known for its *arpillera* crafters.

LITERATURE

Chilean culture and creativity find expression in many fields in addition to visual arts. Literature is a field in which Chileans have made a great contribution. Although composed by a Spanish poet, the epic historic work *La Araucana* is a major part of Chile's cultural heritage. It depicts the bravery and nobility of both the Spanish and American Indian fighters in battle with each other. Its significance is indicated by Castillo-Feliú in *Culture and Customs of Chile:*

> *La Araucana* is an epic poem that lacks the single hero associated with the genre. On the other hand, two abstract heroes stand out: the Spaniard and the Araucanian. This dual hero was to be profoundly imprinted in the national psyche, forging a lasting image of Chileans as composed of the best of two distinct cultures which, together, would mold a new nation.[10]

Chile's literary tradition was furthered in the nineteenth century by Andrés Bello. An academic, government official, and journalist, Bello composed official documents, poems, and essays. Bello composed Chile's national civil code and wrote about Spanish language and culture. Although Bello expressed appreciation for the beauty of the South American landscape, he also praised Chile's Spanish heritage and sought to preserve Spanish culture and tradition in Latin America, even as independent nations emerged from the

LA ARAUCANA

Alonso de Ercilla y Zúñiga was well educated and comfortably positioned among Europe's nobility when he traveled to Chile in 1556. Ercilla had served under a Spanish crown prince and had traveled throughout Europe associating with the royal family members of many nations. Yet he chose to go to Chile and fight in an expeditionary force meant to counterattack the Mapuches, who had just defeated and killed the Spanish governor Valdivia.

Ercilla's high upbringing and cultured education enabled him to be objectively analytical and philosophical even when experiencing fierce battle. The following lines from *La Araucana*, translated by Walter Owen, show how Ercilla was able to appreciate the strength and bravery of the Mapuche warriors, even though they were his battle adversaries:

All Chile trembles at Arauco's name.

What need more words? Such was the hardy race

That o'er the greater part of Chilean soil

Held sway, pre-eminent in deeds and fame,

Whose high renown rang to her farthest bounds,

And that, as I should tell, cost Spain so dear,

And for a season held her arms in check.

A Mapuche musician beats his drum during a festival in Santiago.

old colonies. Later Chilean writers advocated reform and raised awareness of the hardship and suffering within the nation. In the twentieth century, short story writer Baldomero Lillo wrote about the harsh living and working conditions of coal miners, among whom he himself had lived and worked. Lillo's writing is credited with helping to make Chile's leaders and people aware of the social conditions within their country, which in turn led to the great progressive reform efforts undertaken in Chile in the twentieth century.

Two Chilean poets have won the Nobel Prize for literature. In 1945 Gabriela Mistral became the first Spanish American and the first woman writing in the Spanish language, as well as the first Chilean, to win the award. Early in her life Mistral lost the man she loved to a suicide, and this tragedy was reflected in her writing. However, she also wrote many spiritual poems, and love for humanity and compassion for human suffering are frequent themes in her poetry. These virtues are reflected in her 1920s composition *"Ternura"* ("Tenderness"). Chilean poet Pablo Neruda won the Nobel Prize in 1971. He gained initial fame for works rooted in traditional poetic form and common experience. The title of an early work, *Twenty Poems of Love and a Song of Despair*, reflect this period. However, Neruda later wrote about the problems of social and economic injustice he witnessed in traveling the world, and became very visibly associated with the Communist Party in Chile. This brought much controversy to Neruda during the Cold War period, and he was exiled from Chile in 1949. He was able to return to his homeland in 1952 and continued writing in Chile while living in Isla Negra. That location provided inspiration for the aptly named *Memorial de Isla Negra*, a five-volume work published in 1964. Much of the poetry in *Memorial de Isla Negra* reflected upon Neruda's lifetime. In the poem "Exile" he laments upon the time he was forced to leave Chile and the sadness he felt in spite of the fame and recognition he had gained as a poet:

It seemed better to me, the poor earth

of my country—crater, sand

the mineral face of the deserts—

than the glass filled with light they toasted me with.

I felt lost and alone in the garden.[11]

Politics continued to play a large role in Chilean literature throughout the twentieth century. Novelist Isabel Allende is a niece of slain president Salvador Allende. She rose to prominence through the publication of her works *The House of the Spirits* and *Of Love and Shadows*. The first deals with social and political conditions in Chile during the years leading up to and immediately following the military coup. Allende herself went into exile after the coup, and *The House of the Spirits* is influenced by her own experiences. *Of Love and Shadows* dealt with political violence perpetuated against one family under Pinochet. In her later works Allende moved away from her roots, using settings and writing about topics far removed from the politics of Chile and her experiences there. Two of her more recent novels, *Paula* and *Daughter of Fortune*, are both set in California, where Allende moved in the 1970s after first taking exile in Venezuela.

MUSIC

Like Chilean visual artists and writers, Chilean musical artists have also made notable achievements, both in the

IL POSTINO

Pablo Neruda was the subject of a 1990s Italian film entitled *Il Postino* (*The Postman*). It was nominated for best picture at the U.S. Academy Awards in 1996. The film depicted a friendship Neruda developed while living on an Italian island after being exiled from Chile in the 1940s. The friendship is with a postal carrier who delivered his mail on the island and was so enamored of Neruda that he, in spite of being only semiliterate, took up poetry himself.

Il Postino was exceptionally successful in the United States for a foreign language film. In early 1996 it set the record for being the most widely distributed foreign language film in the United States, showing on 250 screens nationwide. The movie also set the U.S. record for the most money ever taken in by a foreign language film, earning over $21.8 million total in theaters.

Neruda was already a world-renowned poet when the movie was released, but he gained even greater fame thereafter. Many more people, especially in Europe and North America, discovered his work as a result of the movie.

Chilean poet Pablo Neruda arrives on the island of Capri in 1952.

TRIBUTES TO NEW SONG ARTISTS

Violeta Parra and Victor Jara, the two biggest stars of the Chilean New Song genre, were well loved during their lifetimes but had only limited public followings. They have come to be much more appreciated posthumously, because of their political consciousness raising as well as their musical talent.

Parra's and Jara's greater fame has been helped by tributes made to them by other popular musical artists. Chilean concert pianist Roberto Bravo recorded a disc consisting of piano performances based on their work. The CD, entitled *A mis amigos* (*To My Friends*), received international acclaim and introduced many new music fans to the Chilean folk artists.

Two popular 1980s rock bands also paid tribute to Victor Jara, commemorating his execution during the 1973 military coup. The band U2 sang about Jara in the song "One Tree Hill" on *The Joshua Tree* album. During a nationally televised concert in Chile in 1987, the band had family members of The Disappeared—those taken by the government and whose whereabouts were not known—on stage with them as lead singer Bono challenged Pinochet to reveal what had happened to the sons, brothers, and other loved ones that had been taken from those on the stage. The band Simple Minds released an album in 1989 called *Street Fighting Years* that dealt with political issues ranging from racial discrimination in South Africa to civil and religious conflict in Northern Ireland, and the album was dedicated to Victor Jara. The title track told the story of the night in Santiago when Jara was taken to the soccer stadium by the military forces staging the coup, and the song paid homage to the beauty of his words and music.

classical and in the traditional forms of music known and appreciated by the early European settlers, and in folk music that has arisen from the culture and styles that have evolved within Chile. Prominent among Chilean classical composers are Domingo Santa Cruz, who wrote many chamber and symphonic pieces, and Alfonso Letelier, who wrote chamber and vocal pieces, and is the most famous among the few Chilean composers who have created operatic works. The Symphonic Orchestra of the University of Chile was formed in 1920 and is recognized as a top-quality orchestra in Latin America. Claudio Arrau, a Chilean native who relocated to Berlin, Germany, at a young age, has gained worldwide fame as a classical pianist and keyboard player. He has won international awards for his renditions of compositions by Beethoven, Chopin, Schumann, and Liszt.

The folk music of Chile is rich and original. Andean folk music, performed in several nations in South America, uses a variety of interesting instruments derived from the native Indian cultures. Among these are pipes called *zamponas*, which are composed from bamboo and come in a wide variety of sizes and combinations to produce various tones. Wind instruments bear resemblances to walking canes and turtle shells, and a percussive instrument called a *palo de lluvia* produces a background sound like steady rainfall. One Chilean band that became very popular making Andean music is Inti Illimani, who relocated to Europe after establishing an international following in the 1970s. Other Chilean folk music artists have, like folk musicians elsewhere, employed modern instruments such as the guitar in their music. The group Huasos Quincheros has been popular in Chile and much of the rest of the world for over half a century. Their music typifies Chilean folk music in that they use the nation's history, culture, and natural beauty as focal points for many of their songs. Such was the case with their well-known "*Chile lindo*," or "Beautiful Chile."

Folk musicians became increasingly political in the later twentieth century. Led by singer Violeta Parra, a movement known as Nueva Canción, or Chilean New Song, developed that endorsed strongly liberal political ideas and social reforms. Parra gained international attention before taking her life in 1967. One song of hers that was especially noteworthy was "*Gracias a la vida*," or "I Give Thanks to Life." Victor Jara was another major performer of New Song music. Songs of his such as "The Right to Live in Peace" and "Prayer to a Farmworker" were pointedly political in nature, although Jara wrote and performed songs about a great many topics. Nevertheless, his outspokenness on behalf of left-wing causes and his support of the Allende government made him a target of the Pinochet regime when it came into power. Jara was one of many interned in the national stadium in Santiago, where he was tortured and killed by loyalists of the new military government. His life and experiences have come to symbolize struggle against oppression and tyranny in Chile.

DANCE

For all of the creative achievements Chile can boast, no cultural characteristic is more important than its national

*Costumed dancers
perform the traditional
cueca in the Plaza de
Armas in downtown
Santiago.*

dance, the *cueca*. The dance is an enactment of a mating ritual and has been described as resembling the cock's courtship of the hen. In formal performances of the *cueca* the man dresses in full *huaso* dress, including black pants, poncho, fringed sash with the red, white, and blue colors of Chile's flag, black felt hat, and black boots with spurs. Women wear dresses or skirts, and both partners wave handkerchiefs as they dance around each other. Instrumental accompaniment is typically by a guitar, harp, accordion, or a combination of instruments, and vocalists often accompany the dancers. Spectators may also add their voices to the music.

THEATER AND FILM

Chile has likewise established itself in the fields of theater and film. Among Chilean playwrights the most revered and successful has been Armando Moock. His 1920 play *La Serpitente* (*The Serpent*), has been performed thousands of times in Latin America and Spain. Overall Moock has written about four hundred theatrical pieces, many of which have had several hundred performances. Egon Wolff is another acclaimed Chilean playwright. His 1962 work *Los Invasores* (*The Invaders)*, is a dramatic political commentary on the plight of the poor and the indifference and uncaring of many wealthy Chileans. Wolff was honored with first prize in the University of Chile's annual theater competition in 1959. This contest annually recognizes achievement in Chilean dramatic theater.

Chilean filmmaking had just started to flourish when Pinochet took over the government in 1973. Government funds that had gone into trying to create a filmmaking legacy and tradition in Chile were cut off, and actors, directors, and producers known to be of leftist political tendencies, of which there were many, fled Chile or were exiled. One exception was Silvio Caiozzi, who produced *Julio Comienza en Julio (Julio Begins in July)* in 1977. That movie enjoyed international popularity and widespread critical acclaim. Director Richard Larrain's *The Borderland* dealt with issues of exile and persecution under the Pinochet regime. Released in 1991, *The Borderland* has received international awards.

The most significant Chilean film ever made may be the 1986 documentary *General Act of Chile*. It was filmed secretly by Miguel Littín, an exiled film director who returned to

Chile to capture daily life there during the Pinochet era. Littín underwent dramatic changes in his appearance and even in his manner of speaking and acting to adopt the persona of a Uruguayan businessman, his alias during the making of the film. Film crews working with Littín received government credentials when they presented themselves as representing film companies in Europe. Remarkably, the film crews were given such free access that they were even able to film inside Pinochet's offices. These adventures were chronicled in a book by Colombian writer Gabriel García Márquez, *Clandestine in Chile*. The movie showed members of Chile's underground in interviews and working against Pinochet, and also showed many negative effects of Pinochet's repression that he tried to keep secret from the rest of the world.

RADIO AND TELEVISION

As in most places in the world, traditional and historic art forms and media have been joined in Chile by modern technological media. Both radio and TV have come to be major elements in everyday life in Chile. Radio stations and formats are as widely varied as they are in North America, playing a range of classical, folk, rock, and pop music, as well as broadcasting news, sports, and talk shows. The largest radio broadcast company in Chile is Radio El Conquistador, which runs eighteen stations in cities throughout Chile.

Chile's largest TV station is Televisión National (TVN), which is, despite its name, not owned by the central government, but privately owned. It broadcasts a wide variety of informational and entertainment programming. The Catholic University in Santiago also operates a TV station that is available throughout the country. With cable and satellite service now commonly available, Chileans are able to view TV from throughout Latin America and the world.

Some of the most popular TV shows in Chile are *telenovelas*. These are similar to daytime soap operas in the United States, but with some differences. *Telenovelas* are broadcast during prime-time evening hours several nights a week and are therefore more widely watched by a wider variety of people than U.S. daytime soap operas usually are. And although soap operas often remain on the air for years or even decades, *telenovelas* run for a limited time, usually several months. The topics and themes covered by *telenovelas* are also more wide-ranging. Family drama and romance are often central to their story lines, but other *telenovelas* have historical settings and recount important events in history. Others deal with important social and political issues, such as the environment and corruption among government officials. *Telenovelas* are produced in many countries and distributed for viewership throughout Latin America. Two popular Chilean *telenovelas* are *Amores de Mercado* and *El Circo de las Montini.*

SPORTS AND ENTERTAINMENT
Besides watching films and TV and listening to radio, Chileans also take pleasure in active pastimes and recreational activities. Some of these are pursued with such enthusiasm and seriousness that they have come to be seen much like art forms, or at least as highly

A Chilean cowboy in full huaso *dress participates in a rodeo. The inset shows one of his boots and spurs.*

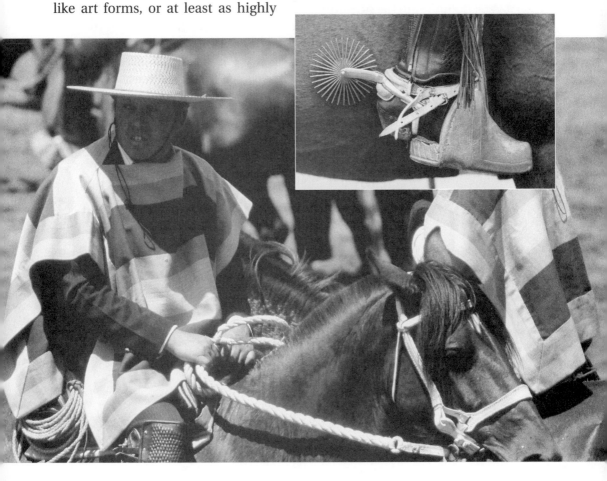

skillful forms of popular entertainment. Kite flying is so popular in Chile that it is sometimes called the national hobby. From spring to the beginning of winter every year, the skies of Santiago are often crowded with kites. While hundreds of thousands of people throughout the country fly kites for fun, a few Chileans hone their kite-flying techniques so finely that they are eligible for membership in the Chilean Kite Fliers Association, which conducts kite competitions and honors those who demonstrate great kite-flying talent.

Among spectator sports, two are highly popular in Chile. One is Chilean rodeo, which has been designated the national sport of Chile. Chilean rodeo is not as rough as North American rodeo—the emphasis is on finesse in riding. Riders and horses try to block a running bull against a fence with precise timing and smooth contact, and audiences appreciate the fine riding. The riders in the Chilean rodeo are called *huasos* after the Chilean cowboys who became legendary for their horseback riding and cattle-herding skills during the early days of colonialism. Rodeo *huasos* dress in traditional garb, including a flat-topped hat, bright red ponchos, fringed pants, and high-rise boots with large spurs. Singing and dancing are also a big part of rodeo festivities.

Rodeo may be deemed the national sport, but no spectator sport is more popular than soccer, which is called football in Latin America. Children play the sport starting at a young age, and local professional and school teams draw enthusiastic crowds of young and old alike. Chile's biggest soccer stars sometimes go on to play for teams in Europe and North America. However, they return to play for the Chilean national team in major competitions such as the World Cup, held every four years. Chile hosted the World Cup in 1962, attracting hundreds of thousands of visitors from around the world. Millions more watched on TV. Chile finished third that year in the competition, its best finish ever. Chile has qualified to compete in the World Cup seven times.

Twenty-First Century Chile

Democracy and freedom of expression have been restored to Chile, and its economy has also shown enduring strength. Yet many problems and challenges face Chile in the early twenty-first century. These include lingering psychological pain for those who suffered under the military dictatorship, adjustment to the strong shift toward globalization that Chile's economy has undergone, and concern over the preservation of a unique Chilean national identity as foreign influences and internationally popular cultural and entertainment styles and trends become increasingly prevalent within Chile.

RESIDUAL PAIN FROM PINOCHET

The inability to put Pinochet on trial has caused frustration and sorrow for the families and friends of those who perished or were persecuted under his rule. These feelings were expressed by a sister of one of The Disappeared in a 2001 *Business Week* article: "For me, finding my brother's remains is a necessity of life. . . . But equally important is knowing and punishing whoever arrested him, tortured him, murdered him, and hid his body."[12]

In late 2003 lawyers representing Pinochet's victims announced they were going to resume prosecution efforts, claiming that he was not showing signs of the physical and mental illnesses for which a Chilean court had exempted him from prosecution. Even though the court's ruling in 2001 specified that Pinochet could be subject to future prosecution if his health improved, those wanting to see Pinochet tried and punished held no great hope or expectation that they would have that satisfaction.

Yet Chileans are divided in their feelings toward Pinochet, and he always maintained a strong base of support among the populace, even at the height of his regime's persecutions. Many Chileans credit him with helping Chile establish long-term economic strength and stability, and believe he prevented the country from becoming an authoritarian Communist state. One way this division among Chileans is manifested is in two different names given to a section of Avenida Providencia, one of Santiago's main streets. Some call the stretch of road Avenida Once de Septiembre (September 11 Avenue). The military government under Pinochet commemorated the coup every year on the anniversary date, and those who supported Pinochet still consider it worthwhile to express appreciation for the events of that day. Those who consider the military coup and Pinochet's government to have been abhorrent call the road Nueva Providencia (New Providence), preferring to look hopefully forward to Chile's future instead of to tragedy in the past.

In August 1999, a group of mothers whose sons disappeared during Pinochet's rule demands that the former dictator be brought to trial.

The manner in which to approach the September 11 date, which continues to be recognized as a holiday, has likewise been a source of disagreement among Chileans. Military

leaders have proposed designating it as a day of reconciliation among Chileans, but not all of the nation's people feel they can easily come to terms with what they experienced under the military dictatorship.

THE NEW ECONOMY

One lasting effect of Pinochet's regime has been the openness of Chile's markets and resources to international interests and heavy dependence that Chile has developed upon trade with other countries. This has led to solid economic growth in Chile overall since the return of civil rule, but there have been rough economic periods as well, either caused or made worse by the dependence upon foreign trade and investment. In a 2001 interview with *Business Week* magazine, Chilean president Ricardo Lagos, who took power in 2000, commented on the state of Chile's economy:

> We had a strong recession with the Asian crisis [of the late 1990s]. But in 2000 we came out of the crisis. . . . This is the most open economy there is. Exports plus imports total more than 50% of gross domestic product. If the U.S. economy slows . . . if Europe is slowing—and everyone knows what's happening in Japan—this could affect our growth a bit.[13]

Lagos's concerns were borne out when Chile's economy remained sluggish through the early 2000s due largely to a worldwide economic slowdown. Unemployment approached 10 percent and growth in national production slowed significantly. Nevertheless, Chile is still relying on heavy trade with major industrial nations for its future economic well-being. In 2003 Chile and the United States finalized a free trade agreement that Chile had been seeking for many years. The agreement allows almost all goods traded between the two countries to avoid tariffs, or import taxes, thereby making it easier for both countries to sell products in the other. Chile has similar agreements with other major nations and groups of nations, including Canada, Mexico, the European Union, and South Korea. Using Chile's highly educated population and good communications facilities to lure Internet, telecommunications, and other high-tech industries to the country is another way in which Chile hopes to create greater economic growth.

POST-PINOCHET GOVERNMENT AND POLITICS

Regardless of how well it does economically, Chile appears to have firmly reestablished its democratic and civil government. Since Pinochet's departure Chile's government structure closely resembles what it was before the coup. An executive branch consists of a president and vice president, elected to serve six years, and a cabinet of ministers appointed by the president. The congress consists of two chambers, a 120-member house of deputies and a 47-member

THE PARANAL OBSERVATORY

Distinctive signs of high technology and modernization can be found throughout Chile. In fact, one of the most advanced pieces of technological equipment in the world can be found in Chile, at the Paranal Observatory, located near Antofagasta in the Atacama Desert. The Very Large Telescope, also known as the VLT, was used to make one of the most impressive astronomical discoveries ever in 2004: a galaxy more than 13 billion light-years away from earth. This was the most distant point in the universe yet seen by humans.

This galaxy was discovered using a process known as gravitational lensing. A gravitational lens is formed when the light from a very distant, bright source (such as a galaxy) "bends" around a massive object (such as another galaxy) that lies between the source and the observer. The new discovery was of one of the earliest galaxies ever formed. In a March 4, 2004, BBC news story, Swiss astronomer Daniel Schaerer said, "What we are observing here are the very first moments of the Universe."

In January 2004, one of four Very Large Telescopes is transported by truck to the Paranal Observatory.

senate, with former presidents who have served at least six years in office designated senators for life. Deputies are elected for four years and senators for eight years. The judicial branch consists of a supreme court, sixteen courts of appeal, and local courts of small claims, major claims, and criminal courts. Chile has thirteen administrative regions, each with its own administrator appointed by the president. Regional councils and town and city officials are chosen in local elections. This form of government has many similarities with others found in democracies and free nations throughout the world.

Along with the restoration of an effective system of representative government, the political divisiveness and factionalism that characterized Chile prior to the 1973 coup also show signs of having returned. In a two-way election for president in January 2000, Lagos, a socialist representing a coalition of leftist parties, defeated Joaquin Lavin, a candidate backed by a centrist-conservative coalition, by only 2 percent. In congressional elections in 2001, the centrist-conservative coalition took control of the senate and made gains in the chamber of deputies, although the Socialists and their allies maintained a narrow majority. There was little expectation that political differences, even sharp ones, would again erupt into armed conflict and tyrannical slaughter, but pronounced political differences among Chileans could make it difficult for the nation to reach consensus in dealing with important issues.

Moreover, political interest and activity appear to be declining among Chile's people. Participation in elections during the 1990s was below levels reached before the 1973 coup and showed no signs of increasing. Author Nick Caistor comments on diminished interest in polities among Chile's people in his book *Chile in Focus: A Guide to the People, Politics, and Culture:*

> In the past . . . Chileans loved to discuss political ideas and affiliations in the way other nations discuss the weather or food. Nowadays, there seems to be almost no interest in politics. . . . This is partly a legacy of the repression of the 1970s and 1980s, when it could be very dangerous to express political opinions. But there is also a widespread feeling that today's party politicians

---

★ FADING PASSIONS OVER PINOCHET

Both during and after the Pinochet regime, Chileans were deeply and bitterly divided in their views of him. While many were appalled over the repressive measures and political persecutions, others were thankful he stopped the confiscation of private property. Some even believed Pinochet prevented Chile from becoming a Communist dictatorship dominated by the Soviet Union.

As the Pinochet era fades further into the past, there are signs that increasingly Chileans are regarding that period with a new attitude: one of indifference. One example is the reaction that documentary filmmaker Patricio Guzman got when he produced *The Pinochet Case*. That film told the story of Pinochet's detainment in London after a warrant for his arrest was issued in Spain and his subsequent return to Chile, where he faced further court proceedings. Guzman had made earlier documentaries about the coup itself—*Battle of Chile* in 1979 and *Chile, Obstinate Memory* in 1996. His work has been well received critically and popular with audiences in much of the world but has had only limited success in Chile, in spite of its focus on issues of direct concern to Chileans. "*Obstinate Memory* ran for four weeks in Santiago and four months in Buenos Aires," Guzman claimed in an October 3, 2002, article in the *New York Times*. "In Santiago *The Pinochet Case* was taken off after three weeks to make room for *Harry Potter.*"

---

are a remote and self-serving elite, distant from the real problems of the populace, who manage to come out on top whatever happens.[14]

Whether Chile will be able to recover from its past and restore its tradition of energetic and progressive political participation among its people was a serious question facing the nation at the start of the twenty-first century.

NATURAL RESOURCES AND PRESERVATION

One political topic that has become of great interest to Chileans recently is environmental protection. With modernization, growth, and an open economy have come serious environmental problems. Air pollution has become a major concern. For years factory and mining emissions contributed to pollution, especially in the Central Valley, where atmospheric conditions cause air to stagnate and pollutants to accumulate and linger. This is especially true during winter, when cold temperatures make the air even more stagnant and smog is an almost constant problem. Pollution in the area around Santiago worsened significantly during the late twentieth century mostly because of greatly increased motor vehicle use and emissions.

The government has responded by taking strong action to try to reduce air pollution. Catalytic converters, mechanisms installed on cars to reduce pollution, are now required on all new cars. Old cars without catalytic converters face restrictions—they are prohibited from driving within Santiago one day a week every week between March and December. During the summer months of January and February, congestion is reduced by the number of people taking vacations from the city, and the air is not as stagnant as it is during the cooler months. Strict emissions controls have also been placed on existing industries within Santiago, and the building of new factories that emit pollutants is prohibited. Air pollution has

A Chilean woman boarding a Santiago bus wears a mask to protect her from the smog of the capital.

been decreased somewhat as a result of these measures, but it will be difficult to continue to make that kind of progress, as the number of vehicles in Santiago, despite restrictions, rose dramatically during the 1990s and continued to do so into the twenty-first century.

Water pollution is another great concern for Chile. For most of the country's history, raw sewage, industrial waste, and pesticide-contaminated runoff entered the water supply untreated. Chile nevertheless managed to maintain a safe and clean supply of drinking water, but action was required to maintain that quality. Many water treatment plants were built at the end of the twentieth century. In the early 2000s environmental advocates sought to get legislation passed that would restrict emissions of industrial waste that had led to serious soil contamination problems. Environmentalists also sought to better regulate hazardous wastes, such as poi-

Environmentalists at an event in Santiago sell T-shirts designed to promote environmental awareness in Chile.

sonous chemicals and nuclear waste, which were very dangerous yet had not been considered a high priority by the government.

Chile's ocean waters are also threatened. These waters provide Chile with one of its most important natural resources: seafood. Like many other industries in Chile, fishing was largely unregulated until the late twentieth century. However, when the numbers of many species of fish declined, Chile's government responded by restricting or forbidding the harvesting of fish and sea animals when their populations became too low. With this kind of intervention, Chile has seen a rebound in the number of *locos*, a kind of shellfish whose numbers dropped alarmingly low in the 1990s. Other marine species have also seen increases in numbers under Chile's policies, but some Chileans would rather take a more comprehensive approach to preserving ocean life, rather than just respond suddenly and urgently when a particular species becomes threatened.

One reason for the large drop in marine populations off the coast of Chile is the new access granted foreign fishing companies starting in the late twentieth century, which has led to great increases in the levels of catches. New access made available to foreigners has also strongly affected Chile's forestry and mining industries. Enormous portions of Chile's forest areas have been transformed from original growth to lumbering, mostly because of the presence of new international lumbering companies in Chile. In *Chile in Focus*, Nick Caistor explains, "Since the late 1970s, Chile's forests have quickly become just another export commodity."[15] Conservationists have tried to preserve portions of what is left of Chile's original growth forests and are particularly concerned about unique local trees, some of which are thousands of years old.

Even copper mining, once considered off-limits to foreigners by most Chileans, has now been made accessible to foreign interests, although Chile still maintains its own national coal mining company with control over most of the mines in the country. Still, the new mining activity undertaken by foreign companies has exacerbated severe pollution problems associated with the coal industry. Besides environmentalists, Mapuche Indian activists have also objected to the infusion of foreign ownership and industrial activity in Chile. They claim the newly arrived international businesses are encroaching upon territory they regard as belonging to the Mapuche, making it more difficult to pursue their property claims in Chilean courts.

SOCIAL ISSUES

In addition to political upheaval and economic uncertainty, the twenty-first century has also brought about major social changes and developments in Chile. A 2002 *New York Times* article said that Chile was "probably the most socially conservative nation in Latin America,"[16] and cited the nation's divorce and abortion laws as examples. Up until 2004 Chile was the only nation in the Western Hemisphere to prohibit divorce. The law was finally changed and divorce was legalized, but because of efforts by the Catholic Church, restrictions have been enacted. If both partners in a marriage want a divorce, they can obtain one only after being separated for a year. If one partner in the marriage objects to the divorce, the minimum separation time is three years before a divorce can be granted.

On abortion, Chile's law remains very strict: Abortion is illegal even to save the life of the mother. Popular support to change the divorce law has been great—70 percent of Chileans favored making it legal according to surveys. But popular demand for legalizing abortion has not been the same, and in the early twentieth century it looked unlikely that changes in Chile's abortion law would be made anytime soon.

Even so, other social changes were occurring in Chile, with or without the church's support. A government-appointed board routinely censored movies in Chile starting in the early twentieth century. Many movies that were popular worldwide were banned for a variety of reasons, usually for sexual or political content, even if it was very mild. Movies by famous directors and producers such as Woody Allen, Oliver Stone, and Federico Fellini were among those censored. Beginning in the early 2000s, the board stopped prohibiting all but the most extremely violent and sexually explicit movies, thus allowing Chileans to be entertained in the same manner as most of the rest of the world. In another sign of a shift away from conservative social attitudes, legislation has been proposed in Chile's congress that would give same-sex

couples many of the same rights as conventional married couples, including insurance and inheritance benefits and hospital visitation rights.

An enormous poster advertising Kodak film towers over shoppers in a Valparaíso mall.

MAINTAINING TRADITION, ADAPTING TO CHANGE

The social, cultural, and political changes occurring in Chile during the 2000s are in many ways typical effects of modernization and internationalism. The influx of new, inexpensive foreign goods, combined with the increased wealth of Chile's people, has resulted in a new emphasis on consumerism in the country and led many Chileans to pursue conspicuous consumption, the practice of acquiring valuable material goods and showing them off to bolster one's image and sense of self-worth. According to Nick Caistor, "This equation of personal value with conspicuous consumption has eaten away at the more traditional notions of solidarity and community which had been deeply rooted in Chile."[17] The influx of foreign stores, restaurants, and other businesses, combined with the increasing presence of foreign movies, music, and TV shows, has caused some Chileans concern about the maintenance and preservation of their traditions and cultural identity.

Still, Chileans by the millions attend rodeos, dance the *cueca* on Independence Day and other holidays, commemorate the battle of Iquique on Navy Day, and stay up until the early morning hours on Christmas Eve preparing and eating outdoor feasts. Others gather to sing and dance for days at a time at the Festival of La Tirana. Chileans still consume empanadas, *porotos granados*, and conger eel in great quantities. The traditional Indian drink yerba maté remains a popular beverage, while Chilean New Song music continues to reach a wide audience within the nation. Although Chile will likely continue to be influenced and affected by modernity and globalization, there is good reason to feel reassured that the country will also maintain the unique characteristics so central to its national identity.

FACTS ABOUT CHILE

GEOGRAPHY

Area: 292,135 square miles (756,626 square kilometers)

Bordering countries: Argentina, Bolivia, Peru

Climate: The north is arid and contains the world's driest desert; the center is temperate with moderate precipitation; cool and moist conditions prevail in the south

Terrain: Low mountains lie along or near the coast through most of the country, the central longitudes are fertile plains, and the eastern part of the country is made up of the Andes Mountains, among the highest in the world, snow-covered peaks and glaciers are present at the highest elevations, the southern part of the country consists of clusters of small islands and peninsulas with a multitude of narrow sea inlets penetrating sheer, towering mountain slopes

Elevation extremes:
Lowest point: Pacific Ocean, sea level
Highest point: Nevado Ojos del Salado, 22,572 feet (6,885 meters)

Natural resources: copper, molybdenum, nitrates, iron, oil, natural gas

Land use:
Arable land: 2.65 percent
Permanent crops: 0.42 percent
Other: 96.93 percent (1998 est.)

Natural hazards: Because it lies along the rim of the Pacific Ocean within a geologically active area known as the Ring of Fire, earthquakes, volcanic eruptions, and tsunamis (tidal waves) all present persistent threats throughout Chile

Environmental issues: Air pollution in the large cities, particularly in Santiago from vehicle emissions; environmental damage from mining, deforestation, and the depletion of rare trees unique to the region; water pollution and its adverse effects on Chile's fish and seafood industry

PEOPLE

Population: 15.7 million (July 2003 est.)

Age structure:
0–14 years: 26.3 percent (male 2,112,251; female 2,018,099)
15–64 years: 66 percent (male 5,151,551; female 5,180,607)
65 years and over: 7.7 percent (male 499,441; female 703,267)
(2003 est.)

Population growth rate: 1.05 percent (2003 est.)

Birth rate: 16.1 births/1,000 population (2003 est.)

Death rate: 5.63 deaths/1,000 population (2003 est.)

Infant mortality rate: 8.88 deaths/1,000 live births (2003 est.)

Life expectancy at birth: Total population: 76.35 years

Total fertility rate: 2.09 children born/woman (2003 est.)

Ethnic groups:
    White and white-Amerindian: 95 percent
    Amerindian: 3 percent

Religion:
    Roman Catholic: 77 percent
    Protestant: 13 percent
    Other religion or not religious: 10 percent

Official language: Spanish

Literacy: 95 percent

Workforce: 5.9 million (2000 est.)
    Agriculture: 14 percent
    Industry: 27 percent
    Services: 59 percent (1997 est.)

GOVERNMENT

Country name: Republic of Chile

Government type: Republic

Capital: Santiago (population 4.7 million in the city, 5.5 million in the metropolitan area)

Administrative divisions: Thirteen regional districts

Date of independence: April 5, 1818

Executive branch: The president is elected by the popular vote to a six-year term and is not eligible for a second consecutive term, the cabinet is appointed by the president

Legislative branch: Bicameral congress; 120-member chamber of deputies and 48 permanent-member senate, former presidents who have served at least six years in office are also deemed senators for life

Judicial branch: Supreme court, sixteen courts of appeals, local civil and criminal courts, judges on the supreme court and courts of appeals are selected by the president from candidates submitted by the sitting members of the courts

ECONOMY

Gross domestic product (GDP): 156.1 billion (2002 est.)

GDP growth rate: 2.1 percent

GDP per capita: $10,100

Population below poverty line: 21 percent (1998 est.)

Inflation rate: 2.5 percent (2002 est.)

Labor force: 5.9 million (2000 est.)

Unemployment rate: 9.2 percent (2002 est.)

Budget:
  Revenues: $17 billion (2001 est.)
  Expenditures: $17 billion (2001 est.)

Industries: copper, other minerals, foodstuffs, fish processing, iron and steel, wood and wood products, transport equipment, cement, textiles

Agricultural products: wheat, corn, grapes, beans, sugar beets, potatoes, fruit, beef, poultry, wool, fish, timber

Exports: copper, fish, fruits, paper and pulp, chemicals

Imports: consumer goods, chemicals, motor vehicles, fuels, electrical machinery, heavy industrial machinery, food

Currency: peso

Notes

Introduction: Chile: A Tale of People and Power

1. John Charles Chasteen, *Born in Blood and Fire: A Concise History of Latin America.* New York: W.W. Norton, 2001, p. 287.

Chapter 1: The Continent's Edge

2. Rex A. Hudson, ed., *Chile: A Country Study.* Washington, DC: Library of Congress Federal Research Division, 1994, p. 68.

3. Simon Collier, Harold Blakemore, and Thomas E. Skidmore, eds., *The Cambridge Encyclopedia of Latin America and the Caribbean.* Cambridge, UK: Cambridge University Press, 1985, p. 21.

4. Ben Box, *Footprint South American Guide 2003.* Bath, UK: Footprint, 2002, p. 636.

Chapter 2: Ancient Empires, Spanish Colonialism, and Early Independence

5. Guillermo I. Castillo-Feliú, *Culture and Customs of Chile.* Westport, CT: Greenwood, 2000, p. 41.

6. Hudson, *Chile: A Country Study*, pp. 23–24.

Chapter 3: Growth, Progress, and Despair: A Century of Contrast

7. Collier, Blakemore, and Skidmore, *The Cambridge Encyclopedia of Latin America*, p. 248.

8. Simon Collier and William F. Slater, *A History of Chile, 1808–1994.* Cambridge, UK: Cambridge University Press, 1996, p. 307.

CHAPTER 4: CHILE'S PEOPLE AND THEIR LIFESTYLES

9. Castillo-Feliú, *Culture and Customs of Chile*, pp. 87–88.

CHAPTER 5: CULTURE, THE ARTS, AND ENTERTAINMENT

10. Castillo-Feliú, *Culture and Customs of Chile*, p. 109.

11. Ilan Stavans, ed., *The Poetry of Pablo Neruda*, trans. Alastair Reid. New York: Farrar, Straus and Giroux, 2003, p. 698.

CHAPTER 6: TWENTY-FIRST CENTURY CHILE

12. Quoted in Louise Egan, "Chile's Disappeared: Will the Search Ever End?" *BusinessWeek* Online, February 12, 2001. www.businessweek.com.

13. Quoted in *Business Week* International Editions, Latin America, "A Socialist Who's Betting on the New Economy," April 2, 2001, p. 25.

14. Nick Caistor, *Chile in Focus: A Guide to the People, Politics, and Culture.* Brooklyn, NY: Interlink, 1998, p. 54.

15. Caistor, *Chile in Focus*, p. 44.

16. Larry Rohter, "After Banning 1,092 Movies, Chile Relaxes Its Censorship," *New York Times*, December 13, 2002, p. A7.

17. Caistor, *Chile in Focus*, p. 53.

CHRONOLOGY

14,000 B.C.
Nomadic Indians inhabit the region comprising Chile.

8000–1000
The Chinchorro, a semisedentary people, thrive in Chile and become the dominant civilization in the area.

A.D. 200
The Mapuche start to emerge as a distinctive tribe.

1475
Inca invasion of Chile results in a short-lived conquest of the northern part of the country.

1520
Ferdinand Magellan sails around the southern tip of South America along the coast of Chile, becoming the first known European to sight Chile's land.

1535
Diego de Almagro leads first Spanish exploration of Chilean territory.

1540–1541
Pedro de Valdivia leads conquest and settlement of Chile for Spain, founding what will become the national capital, Santiago, in the Central Valley.

1553
Mapuche uprising led by Chief Lautaro results in the destruction of a Spanish fort at Tupacel and the killing of Valdivia.

1557
Lautaro is killed by Spanish fighters.

1558
Mapuche uprising is put down, but the Mapuche remain effectively in control of southern Chile until the late nineteenth century.

1560s
Alonso de Ercilla y Zúñiga composes *La Araucana*, an epic poem that becomes a major part of Chile's cultural heritage.

1759–1796
Chile is granted greater independence from the rule of the viceroyalty of Peru under the leadership of the Bourbon family in Spain.

1807
French leader Napoleón Bonaparte conquers Spain, forcing Spanish colonies throughout the world, including Chile, to decide whether to remain loyal to Spain.

1810
Chile declares itself independent from Spain until such time as the deposed Spanish monarch, Ferdinand VII, is restored to the throne.

1814
Spanish troops reconquer Chile in the battle of Racagua; fighters for Chilean independence such as Bernardo O'Higgins flee the country to continue the fight for independence from abroad.

1817
O'Higgins and Argentine independence leader José de San Martin defeat the Spanish in the battle of Chacabuco. O'Higgins is named supreme director of Chile.

1818
A provisional constitution is adopted.

1822
O'Higgins devises the first permanent Chilean constitution, bestowing great and concentrated powers upon himself. This sets off a reaction against O'Higgins that results in his leaving office.

1823–1830
Civil war between liberals and conservatives ends with a conservative victory in the battle of Lircay.

1833
Diego Portales implements a new government and constitution.

1836–1839
Chile defeats a confederation of Peru and Bolivia in a war
that culminates with land and sea battles in January 1839,
both of which are won resoundingly by Chile.

1850s
The presidency of Manuel Montt is twice challenged by attempted rebellions and by renewed hostilities with the Mapuche, who continue to effectively control the south of Chile.

1874
Property ownership requirements for eligibility to vote in
elections are eliminated, and voting rights are extended to
all literate adult males.

1879–1883
Chile again confronts Peru and Bolivia militarily in the War
of the Pacific. Chile is again victorious.

1891
President José Manuel Balmaceda is forced out of office by
military forces loyal to members of congress.

Early 1900s
Increased attention to and awareness of the plight of Chile's
poor leads to growing support for socially progressive gov-
ernmental policies.

1920
Arturo Alessandri is elected president, having run on a reformist, populist platform.

1925
Alessandri drafts a new constitution, ratified in a popular
vote, that restores major powers to the presidency and also
provides for direct election of the president and members
of congress by the people. Voting rights are extended to all
men over eighteen.

1932
Alessandri is elected for another term. Major progressive
social reform efforts are undertaken in Chile.

1945
Chilean Gabriela Mistral becomes the first South American
writer to win the Nobel Prize for Literature.

1948
Contrary to Chile's legacy of political tolerance, President Gabriel González Videla outlaws the Communist Party.

1949
Women are granted the right to vote in Chile.

1958
A new political party spearheaded by moderately progressive Catholic leaders, the Christian Democrats, shows impressive strength in its first-ever national election.

1964
Led by Eduardo Frei, the Christian Democrats win the presidency by a wide margin. The new government undertakes major social reform efforts.

1970
Socialist Salvador Allende is elected president in a sharply fragmented three-way election. Allende implements sweeping economic and social changes. Strong opposition to Allende, both within the country and from without, steadily mounts.

1971
Pablo Neruda becomes the second Chilean poet to win the Nobel Prize for Literature.

1973
Allende and his Socialist government are overthrown in a bloody military uprising that results in the seizure of power by army general Augusto Pinochet. Strict authoritarian rule is imposed and political opponents are persecuted, with many killed or made to vanish with no trace.

1982
After responding well to new conservative policies introduced by Pinochet, the Chilean economy suffers severe recession and inflation. Dependence upon foreign aid forces the military government to begin to act to restore democracy and political freedoms.

1988
In a national vote, the Chilean people choose to end Pinochet's regime and restore the elective democratic form

of government they had before the military coup in 1973.
Pinochet steps down in 1990.

1998
While traveling in England, Pinochet is detained by authorities after a Spanish judge issues a warrant for his arrest, but he is eventually released for health reasons.

2001
Chilean courts effectively thwart efforts to prosecute Pinochet for atrocities his regime committed by ruling that he is mentally and physically unfit to stand trial.

2003
The United States and Chile finalize a major free trade agreement.

2004
Chile becomes the last nation in the Western Hemisphere to legalize divorce.

FOR FURTHER READING

BOOKS

Martyn Bramwell, *Central and South America*. Minneapolis, MN: Lerner, 2000. Part of the World in Maps series. Heavily illustrated, colorful, fact-filled, and easy to read.

Sylvia McNair, *Chile*. New York: Childrens Press, 2002. Explores the geography, history, society, and culture of Chile.

David Schaffer, *South America*. Berkeley Heights, NJ: MyReportLinks.com/Enslow, 2004. Presents an overview of the geography, history, peoples, and natural life of the continent. Includes extensive references to related Internet sources.

Anna Selby, *Argentina, Chile, Paraguay, Uruguay*. Austin, TX: Raintree Steck-Vaughn, 1999. General information on Chile and its Latin American neighbors.

Charles J. Shields, *Chile*. Philadelphia: Mason Crest, 2004. General information on Chile with a special focus on current events and issues. Easily readable; includes many photos and tables.

Sarah Wheeler, *Travels in a Thin Country: A Journey Through Chile*. New York: Modern Library, 1994. For advanced readers. A personal travelogue of the author's journey from one end of Chile to the other in the early 1990s. Touches upon historical and political information and issues.

Jane Cohen Winter and Susan Roraff, *Chile*. Tarrytown, NY: Benchmark/Marshall Cavendish, 2002. An overview of the country with extensive information on the nation's government, economy, environment, and society.

WEB SITES

Geographia (www.geographia.com/chile). Contains geographical, historical, and cultural information, as well as travel advice on a calendar of events.

Lonely Planet (www.lonelyplanet.com/destinations/south_america/chile_and_easter_island). Plenty of background and travel information on Chile, with a clickable map that provides detailed information on specific regions.

WORKS CONSULTED

BOOKS

Ben Box, *Footprint South American Guide 2003.* Bath, UK: Footprint, 2002. Part of a travel guide series that includes cultural and historical information on each country in addition to detailed descriptions of places of interest and practical travel information.

Nick Caistor, *Chile in Focus: A Guide to the People, Politics, and Culture.* Brooklyn, NY: Interlink, 1998. A concise and insightful exploration of Chile. Includes practical travel and sightseeing information as well as essential facts and statistics.

Guillermo I. Castillo-Feliú, *Culture and Customs of Chile.* Westport, CT: Greenwood, 2000. Covers many aspects of Chilean society and history, with an emphasis on the arts, cultural heritage, and characteristics of the country.

John Charles Chasteen, *Born in Blood and Fire: A Concise History of Latin America.* New York: W.W. Norton, 2001. A history of the social, cultural, and political aspects of the entire Latin American world from the time of the Spanish discovery of America until the end of the twentieth century.

Simon Collier, Harold Blakemore, and Thomas E. Skidmore, eds., *The Cambridge Encyclopedia of Latin America and the Caribbean.* Cambridge, UK: Cambridge University Press, 1985. A comprehensive study of the entire region of Latin America.

Simon Collier and William F. Slater, *A History of Chile, 1808–1994.* Cambridge, UK: Cambridge University Press, 1996. A detailed history of the country from the time of independence until the 1990s. Includes extensive statistical data and tables.

Pamela Constable and Arturo Valenzuela, *A Nation of Enemies: Chile Under Pinochet*. New York: W.W. Norton, 1991. Recounts Pinochet's rise to power and the history of Chile during his regime.

Alonso de Ercilla y Zúñiga, *La Araucana: The Epic of Chile*. Vol. 1. Trans. Walter Owen. Buenos Aires: Walter Owen, 1945. An English translation of the historic poem, with additional Spanish poetry translations and critical works.

Gabriel García Márquez, *Clandestine in Chile: The Adventures of Miguel Littín*. New York: Henry Holt, 1986. Chronicles the shooting of the films made by Littín during the time he returned from exile disguised as a foreigner. The book was written from interviews that García Márquez, a Nobel Prize winner, conducted with Littín.

Rex A. Hudson, ed., *Chile: A Country Study*. Washington, DC: Library of Congress Federal Research Division, 1994. One in a series of country reports by the Library of Congress; provides a geographic, historic, economic, and sociological overview of Chile.

Ilan Stavans, ed., *The Poetry of Pablo Neruda*. Trans. Alastair Reid. New York: Farrar, Straus and Giroux, 2003. A comprehensive collection of Neruda's work, spanning his entire writing career.

Barbara A. Tanenbaum, "Telenovelas." In *Encyclopedia of Latin American History and Culture*. Vol. 5, ed. Barbara A. Tenenbaum. New York: Charles Scribner's Sons/Macmillan Library Reference, 1996. A comprehensive multivolume set covering a wide variety of topics pertaining to Latin America.

Edwin Williamson, *The Penguin History of Latin America*. London: Allen Lane/Penguin, 1992. A deep and thorough history of Latin America from the time of the arrival of the Spanish. Includes a chapter specifically on Chile in the twentieth century.

PERIODICALS

Business Week International Editions, Latin America, "A Socialist Who's Betting on the New Economy," April 2, 2001.

Alan Riding, "Arts Abroad: Telling Chile's Story, Even if Chile Has Little Interest," *New York Times*, October 3, 2002.

Larry Rohter, "After Banning 1,092 Movies, Chile Relaxes Its Censorship," *New York Times*, December 13, 2002.

Geri Smith, "A Giant Step Toward Free Trade Across the Americas?" *Business Week*, June 16, 2003.

INTERNET SOURCES

BBC News, UK Edition, "Telescope Probes Far Off Galaxy," March 4, 2004. http://news.bbc.co.uk/1/hi/sci/tech/352 5701.stm.

Louise Egan, "Chile's Disappeared: Will the Search Ever End?" *BusinessWeek* Online, February 12, 2001. www.business week.com.

Facts On File World News Digest, "Facts on Ricardo Lagos Escobar," January 20, 2000. www.facts.com.

INDEX

PICTURE CREDITS

Cover photo: © Pablo Corral V/CORBIS
© Carlos Barria/CORBIS, 85
Chris Barton/Lonely Planet Images, 27
Chris Beall/Lonely Planet Images, 25
© Bettman/CORBIS, 8, 41, 45, 49
Tom Cockrem/Lonely Planet Images, 5
© CORBIS, 30
© Corel Corporation, 18
© Pablo Corral V/CORBIS, 54, 56, 58, 67, 86, 89
© European Southern Observatory (ESO), 13, 82
© Macduff Everton/CORBIS, 15
© Kevin Fletcher/CORBIS, 64
Getty Images, 71
© Peter Guttman/CORBIS, 74
© Hulton/Archive by Getty Images, 26
Chris Jouan, 10, 20
© Craig Lovell/CORBIS, 16, 22
© Charles O'Rear/CORBIS, 77
© Photo Collection Alexander Alland, Sr./CORBIS, 39
© PhotoDisc, 21, 23
Reuters/CORBIS, 50, 69, 80
© Paul A. Souders/CORBIS, 77 (inset)
© Hubert Stadler/CORBIS, 61
Brent Winebrenner/Lonely Planet Images, 62
Woods Wheatcroft/Lonely Planet Images, 11

ABOUT THE AUTHOR

David Schaffer has edited and designed books and magazines for young readers for the past nineteen years. A graduate of Skidmore College and the New York University Publishing Institute, he has written books, magazine articles, and newspaper features on history, geography, entertainment, travel, politics, and social problems confronting young people.

Schaffer lives in upstate New York with his wife, Nancy, and two daughters, Helena and Lily Jane.